AutobyBobraphy
volume VII

Feather dust, a gardener's confess_____

Bob Flowerdew, Dickleburgh 2024

Feather dust, a gardener's confessions

It's not your height that matters so much as the height of those around you...

When I started gardening for a living it seemed the field was already rather full: with actors, musicians, painters and other handymen. Folk who had likewise taken up gardening as another string in a somewhat threadbare bow. Many were doing a fair enough job but others practiced seemingly random workmanship, with some displaying an amazing lack of basic knowledge. Thus mostly because the competition was so poor my initially slightly-less-than-incompetent service was to prove more than adequately sufficient by local standards.

Naturally as with most businesses it was slow finding my first clients, especially living in a rural county with a small rather spread out population. However this was an ageing population, many living surrounded by gardens once well tended by now departed husbands. Daunted by the workload to keep these respectable many were desperate for any help, apparently. And in rural areas 'word' for good or bad gets around astonishingly rapidly. Before long I'd picked up enough clients to keep me busy, at least during the warmer months when lawns, hedges and weeds were growing full pelt.

At first it was hard to find enough employment to fill the winter months, which suited me to some extent as I was already writing. However in the garden much work needs be done during the better weather in winter, indeed much important work is done, particularly make-overs with most things moving, tree and shrub planting and so on.

Some folks don't appreciate that maintaining most attractive gardens requires many small tasks performing throughout the year not just a quick blitz the week before they have a barbecue. I partly hold TV garden makeover programs responsible for this 'you can get it all done in a day / weekend' delusion. Fortunately I was able to find and satisfy enough clients to grow a viable year round business, though some were hard to convince at first, thanks to the poor service offered by the 'competition'.

Mauvaises herbes

One prospective client grilled me unexpectedly thoroughly before taking me on. This was an odd cross examination, for this lady, a retired teacher, had some years before tried to educate me in French, a subject let's say I was a little less than fluent in. She was now demanding I identify, one by one, a dozen or so of her, fairly common, shrubs and herbaceous plants about her garden. Well I passed, and she revealed why she'd asked. First she'd remembered I was a bookish kid so wondered how come I was taking up such a mundane, physical and not intellectual career. And secondly, and much more importantly, because for some unfathomable reason the previous alleged gardener had, instead of a proper 'weeding' dug out every plant in a large border, piled these in a mound behind the garden shed, and left leaving nothing in the bed but the Ground Elder, a common pervasive weed. This did not seem to have been in anger or revenge but more an act of despair. I suspected he'd commenced on the work whilst not understanding it sufficiently to either perform this task correctly or at the correct time of year. Then realising his error had done a runner rather than be embarrassed confronted by his foolishness. Needless to say I did not make the same error and set about negotiating a lifetime's employment battling with her Ground Elder on a fortnightly basis

How not to plant trees
Similarly badly served were a young couple who had commissioned another local 'gardener' to make them a mini orchard. They had been supplied with, the 'traditional' and poor, selection of Bramley's Seedling (the cooker, gets too big a tree and in season they're everywhere for the asking), Cox's Orange Pippin (probably The best dessert apple, but also a very miffy grower hard to crop), and James Grieve (a good early but one that's gone pappy the day after picking). All three had been planted by this so called gardener, and all had looked fine, till the following mid summer when they went down hill and withered to dead sticks.

I was called in, I was happy to advise them, indeed relishing it as I had already came across similar on several occasions, indeed was dining out on it. Anyway, went up to the dead trees, their withered leaves were still hanging on (a very bad sign as when these drop off there's often still some small hope). The trees were staked, I loosened the ties and with no effort pulled those up, then as easily lifted the trees straight out. Their roots came up intact, still in the perfect shape of the tubs they'd originally been grown in, with a dusting of bone dry peat. On examination each tree had been plonked in its hole, a stake driven through the root-ball and the hole re-filled, without the roots being teased and spread out. Worse, rather than repacking soil around the root-balls the genius had packed in ridiculous quantities of peat which he had neither mixed in nor pre-dampened. (Possibly this pointless waste was inspired by advertisements from an earlier time promoting bales of peat as 'soil improvers', mostly derived from the then popular fashion for so called low maintenance heather beds and minlature conifer gardens which rather liked a load of peat in their soil and even more as a weed suppressing mulch on top.)

These hapless trees had survived initially on their reserves, managed to produce leaves, flowers, and then had withered as their roots were neither ever watered sufficiently, if at all, nor were able to penetrate out through the several inches of powder dry peat. This was actually a classic problem, with or without the peat, repeated all over the country from when container grown trees were introduced. Folk planted skimpily without teasing the roots out thus many trees would look okay for a while then fade away or simply look miserable until they could get some roots to grow out from the root-ball. However they seldom fared well, and the encircled congested root-ball gave little grip so the trees could just fall over when cropping heavily or during gales. Then by also adding so much peat all round encasing the root-balls in an arid barrier this 'gardener' had further ensured these trees would certainly fail.

I dug their sites over mixing the peat in and watering heavily as I did so (with some detergent washing up liquid to help). Later in autumn when the soil had settled I planted a more suitable selection of bare rooted trees, these are usually better at establishing as their root system is larger and well shaped so can be properly consolidated in the ground. I chose them Discovery, one of the best 'Earlies', a delicious Brownlee's Russet for early winter, and Winston a tasty long keeper. Needless to say I also ensured these were watered regularly their first spring and summer, and I took time to go back and carefully de-fruited them that first summer. It really is best practice to allow a tree or bush a year or more to establish before allowing it any crop, leaving a full crop can even stunt growth for many years to come. It's okay to leave just a couple of fruits to ripen so you can be sure these are true to variety, but otherwise patience is strictly required.

A cut above
Anyway, I was a keen amateur, neither especially knowledgeable nor that highly skilled. However gardening, especially jobbing or maintenance gardening, is in essence simple enough and not unlike the farm work I'd grown up with. Thus as I said I reckon I gained my reputation as a green fingered gardener more from doing the job attentively rather than knowledge or skill. It's not what you do or how hard the job is but how it looks to them when you've finished! And your work can look even better when you are following a string of far worse gardeners.

What surprised many clients was what a neat job I managed in the miserly amount of time they were prepared to pay for, especially if they had previously had some other 'gardener' attempting the same. But as I said, it is simple though you need to think about what you are doing. Then once you have an area under control it is relatively easy to maintain- compared to the effort to get there. Anyway there are books full of instructions for every job or plant you're not sure of.

True much of gardening is manual very physical work but many folk make it harder than necessary. Oddly clients thought much of my advantage was from having professional tools, which can indeed make a minute difference. 'Professional' tools are not that different nor essential, but sensible well sharpened tools are, and a mower that will start at will is crucial. It is little saving of effort to have a motorised mower if you have to 'wind it up' for half an hour before beginning to use it!

I had a neighbour who I could hear spending so long pulling the cord he would have been better winding a spring. I reckon some days he took longer trying to start his mower than it then took him to cut his little patch. Now a business has to earn money, has to be time efficient. For example I hated using powered hedge trimmers, they're noisy and dangerous. But few clients will pay you for the longer time it takes to cut a large hedge with shears. Similarly as just noted you really must have a lawnmower that will start when asked!

I repeat. People would say to me "it's easy for you with professional tools". No, it's just damn hard work to use poor ones!

In particular many folk fail to sharpen metal cutting edges. And not just the lawnmower blades which if blunted make harder work for both mower and owner. I sharpen spades, trowels, secateurs as well as my hoes. ALL cutting edges need to be sharpened often or they make hard work. And unsafe work, if they are blunt more force is used and then slips and accidents happen.

And be generous with the oil can; oil wheels on barrows, hinges on doors and windows, locks and catches, oil them and they'll work more easily and endure much longer.

Vegetables make us proud, flowers can make us humble
Now I was self taught, having grown up on a farm I was well used to tasks such as hoeing weeds and trimming hedges, and had used a lawnmower from before I drove tractors. (To my father's distress I once somehow 'pruned' to the ground a six foot copper beech whilst mowing the family orchard.) I'd also long helped aunts and grandfather in their gardens and plots, and had liked tending the crops more than the flowers (mostly from being boy-hungry, somehow the flowers seemed uninteresting, I could see the point of a row of swelling juicy carrots). Now because growing vegetables does require skill and effort we can become proud of our successes. On the other hand flowers somehow do so well, almost magically, so often regardless of our 'help' they help keep us humble with their effortless beauty.

Ie. On the whole maintenance gardening is much 'easier' than growing crops especially vegetables most of which require a considerable degree of preparation, diligent work and good timing. On the other hand cultivating fruit and nut trees and bushes is remarkably agreeable as many crop near unaided year after year almost regardless of your input. Now the up-keep of an already well maintained ornamental garden just to keep it still well maintained falls in between these. It is demanding but most of the tasks are simple, straight forward and repetitive.

Gardening, as with house cleaning, is best considered as comprising two parts, you start with a massive 'Spring clean' but afterwards to be seriously effective it's only regular systematic cleaning that keeps everything pristine. Then as you keep up the iterations it should become much less, or rather less hard, work each time.

Always 'maintain your position' making the good bits better again before moving onto more demanding tasks. For example start by hoeing and weeding those beds and borders that are nearly clean first before tackling the more time consuming overgrown ones.

any fool can make work, takes no talent at all
I have watched folk carry heavy things to their wheelbarrow rather than move it closer. I have seen folk stack such as paving slabs where they will most obviously soon be in the way and need moving again. I have despaired as helping friends out I have stood and waited, again, while they searched for something else that needed bringing but wasn't brought. The much repeated 'failing to plan is planning to fail' is so correct in gardening as everywhere else.

We need to think through tasks, what we are trying to achieve, how we are going to do it, what tools and supplies we need to start, and finish with.

And to do all this before we begin on the ground. Even the more so with landscaping designs, you need imagine how it will grow up over the coming years. You will see your mistakes grow large, a huge advantage of concentrating on vegetables is you can bury any errors each autumn. Likewise pruning, think ahead, it's not what you remove but how it will grow back that needs be in consideration.

Another old well known saying is 'a stitch in time saves nine' which is so true with everything in life particularly gardening. The grass starts to grow in March when it's easy mowing, however if left till April it can be done but you now have hard work and dead patches. Left uncut even longer then by May it becomes a meadow nearly beyond cutting. The same goes week by week throughout the growing period, it's little effort to cut grass that was cut a week or so before, harder if it was two weeks, and downright tough after a month.

Likewise there's 'hoe when you don't see weeds and then you never will.' This is very much so. Most weeds coming from seed are easy to kill when a few days old, or a week or two, but given a month become established and resilient. Hoeing regularly also disrupts seedlings so small you'd barely notice them whereas left till a week later they'd be more obvious.

Gardening success, and certainly in appearance, is much about this frequent repetition, and good timing. Thus my favourite quip of all "There is a right time for everything in gardening and too often it was last week, or worse, last month!"

To maintain their own garden folk can do what ever happens to take their notice at any time, it's their choice, with or without success. A professional gardener however has to satisfy the clients who may well have unrealistic 'Chelsea inspired' delusions and not comprehend the efforts or timings involved.

More over a 'hired to design and install Landscape gardener' will then usually walk away from their mistakes. Though at risk to their reputation, each one is after all a one off. The real problem is they seldom ever consider the maintenance tasks much if at all. Now on the other hand the hands on, jobbing or maintenance gardener will have to return to their mistakes, over and over. Thus if a design unthinkingly requires the lawnmower to be carried over a gravel section or down steps then if and when it can be this will soon get sorted by those having to do the task.

(I believe it was the great Gertrude Jekyll or possibly Sackville-West who placed pillars with turf growing on top on the 'patio' in front of her bedroom windows so these swatches would blend into the lawn beyond. No thought to the poor wretches balancing on top of ladders having to water and close cut these patches all over with hand shears once or twice every week.)

Repetition, repetition, repetition

The most important discipline is to be methodical especially with dozens of gardens to tend each week. Establishing a routine is the solution, especially getting the regular maintenance chores completed before starting on any less frequent or seasonal tasks.

On arrival I'd walk round inspecting each garden noting what needed doing most urgently. (A pocket notebook was immensely handy, and also logged mileage and any sundry jobs to be billed, everyone has a smartphone to do this now.) I'd simultaneously be collecting up and disposing of even the tiniest piece of litter of any derivation (one bit of litter makes an immense difference to the appearance). Plus I'd collect up other junk, tools, toys etc. 'in the way' and put them some appropriate place preferably out of immediate sight. Then I'd sharpen my hoe and weed the beds and borders. Once these were done and raked over I'd trim and dead-head any fading flowers, clip the lawn edges, finally mowing the grass and brushing down the paths. I'd collect all suitable materials for compost, and if the client had no compost bin then bag these to take home, for a small fee of course. These were then added to my compost bins as a staggeringly large source of humus, which my sandy soil then consumed as fast as could be fed it. (If on clay such humus would have been equally useful, it really is The fuel for the garden.)

This was a standard visit, repeated weekly throughout the

growing period. Of course in winter most of those tasks were not necessary though there were plenty of others such as heavier hedging, pruning, and planting projects, indeed whatever you could inspire your customers to be paying for. Slowly I learned that with persuasion many clients could be shown the sense of continuing to have a gardener visit regularly throughout the year. Mostly to keep the place 'spic and span', do winter pruning, plant up new colour or fruit for the next year. But also that my sudden appearance and disappearance was also an effective squatter and burglar deterrent. (This was not an idle, nor a veiled threat, both squatters and burglars look for signs of absence).

Um, that's unusual...
One couple certainly got their money's worth, they'd retained me for a weekly 'Security check and tidy' right through the colder months, mostly as they would be abroad for a long break. (Client's who were away were my ideal, their garden becomes your own, and you do not have to fit in with their routines.) I drove in, parked, and was walking round picking up pieces of windblown litter before doing some planned winter pruning to a large bed of roses. As I poked about I wondered why a deep border at the back of their house seemed so wet. It had been raining recently yet this was a relatively dry border sheltered from the rain on three sides by the house, and it was downright wet indeed muddy. Investigating I

discovered, well hidden behind a large shrub, water seeping down the wall, it seemed to be bubbling out through a crack in the brickwork a couple of feet below a window on the upper floor level, a bathroom I presumed. Made a few calls and had a plumber there in double quick time. If I'd not been there and alert that leak would likely have been running till their return several weeks or months later doing untold damage in and to the house in the process. Needless to say from then on of course I recited this saga to each and every customer I was in the process of endeavoring to enroll.

Sage advice

Simply being methodical, sensible and working with sharp tools I soon annoyed more slovenly competitors whilst I gained some good contracts and lovely gardens. One day I was approached by another older, gardener, one long known in the area for his excellent work. (And for charging a modest amount which was probably more the truth behind his general approval.) Seemed because of ill health he was retiring and was I interested in taking on his clients? He really did not want, as he put it, to expose them, to some of the others in the area and he had seen my neat workmanship maintaining gardens. He was handing his round of clients over to me for nothing, gratis, just so 'his gardens' would still be well looked after (not the clients, his attachment was to the gardens of course).

And he wanted to offer me a bit of advice.

He reckoned I was far too keen and should plan ahead a bit more. He was impressed by my speed, and the neatness I achieved, but reckoned I should think it out more carefully, he posed a question.

"What is the last thing a rat catcher does before leaving?"

"Gets paid" I suggested hopefully.

"Not quite, he puts back a healthy pair just in order to ensure future business!"

He then said "That Doctor's garden you're taking on, the one with the long rose border beside the path right in front of his surgery window, what are you going to do first?"

I replied I'd deadhead those roses, hoe the weeds underneath which were getting away, trim the edges and mow the grass.

"And what will you do the following week?"

I said I'd do much the same.

"And what will happen after several weeks?"

I did not comprehend so he continued. "It's the same for a good cleaner, nobody ever notices what a good job they do as it always looks just the same. See, if you hoe and trim that rose bed every week it'll never look any different. After a while the Doctor will look out and wonder why he pays for a gardener as other than the seasons nothing seems to change. He will start thinking up more jobs that 'need' doing. He particularly wants that old hedge grubbing up at the back. Now you would not want to do that would you?" (A very hard job and one best avoided unless bringing in a back-hoe digger or can pass it on to some naïve sub-contractor.)

"No, no, no, never ever hoe week after week, all the weeds will be gone and no new ones will ever appear. You must pursue other tasks, so you mow the grass and deadhead, prune and tidy weekly but never trim the edges nor hoe that or any other bed every week. For such frequent repetition will ensure no weed or 'scruffiness' will ever show. No, you must only ever hoe and trim any bed every third or fourth week never more often. Then the Doctor may notice how a few weeds emerge the second week, how the edges start to look a little unkempt. By the third week he will have definitely noticed, it looks needy and getting worse. And then you strike and suddenly that bed looks spic and span again. The Doctor is now reassured, the bed was getting away but was put right and looks lovely, and he is so glad he does have a gardener to do it for him."

I was enlightened, but in a quandary. "I like to keep busy and after all they're paying me so how do I fill all the time during the weekly visits then, the Doctor does not have a vegetable plot?

He responded "You divide the garden up so you hoe different beds different weeks" and added "I used to spend hours grubbing out path and lawn weeds by hand." Anyway he likes topiary, now I never let him have any as my wrists would not take the near constant trimming so I suggest you put some along the drive, maybe some more in large vases about the patio as well. He'll really love those, the extra watering and trimming will keep you regularly busy, and his need for you, in full view."

He was so right, and not only on how to keep our clients happy. If you want be get rid of weeds in a bed forever then hoe each and every week, with a sharp hoe, keep it up and soon you'll never see no weeds. But if you want to have to hoe weeds in that bed forever and a day then simply do not hoe quite so frequently.

Narrow escape

That wise old bird also tipped me the wink on one client-from-hell he'd assiduously avoided taking on. This spry old lady lived between two of his clients, two I would be taking on so I was going to bump into her sooner or later. And she was bound to ask me to take on her garden as well for she could not keep a gardener long. He looked at me earnestly "For your sanity's sake do not take her on, I can't say more than that".

Some weeks later I was working away at one of these

clients and as he had predicted the spry old lady popped up and after a little labored small talk then asked if I'd be willing to take her garden on. I pleaded I was over-booked. She insisted. I declined politely several times but eventually allowed her to show me her estate just in case... It was all very neat, just too neat, prissy even. She explained how she kept it up herself but needed more help as she was getting on. She was always getting new gardeners but they were no good and none of them never continued with her very long. (Note of alarm; this is always THE warning sign, if you hear that prior occupants of any job or whatever did not last long make a run for it while you still can.)

I promised her as soon as I had a vacancy...

A few weeks later I was back working away at the same clients' gardens. I watched curiously as another jobbing gardener cycled up to the spry old lady's house, a 'new boy'. A very short while later from the other side of the fence I could hear him being harangued. I peeked, he was not gardening but cleaning her car. And being told off whilst doing so as he'd not cleaned one of the letters on the car's number plate sufficiently spotlessly, and he had to shut the car door as the courtesy light would flat the battery, and to watch his black soled boots did not mark her immaculately scrubbed concrete drive....

I smiled smugly to myself, the old boy had been so right.

Phew, that was a near miss there.

a cut above

As I've noted I preferred to use my own mower, one of many I had accumulated, a rotary usually, mainly as it would <u>start</u> unlike many clients' machines. A rotary can cope with most terrain and levels of undergrowth with it's spinning horizontal 'propeller' blade underneath. When I first started I'd offered a cylinder mower option for those with finer lawns but found it difficult to get folk to pay for this with sufficient regularity. It gets much less easy to use a cylinder mower if the grass gets a tad too long. Grass that's grown up more than an inch or so becomes impossible to mow with a cylinder. With a rotary you simply take a 20" wide cut with a 24" cut mower so the fewer if longer clippings pass through without choking up, though that naturally requires more passes. This does not work the same with a cylinder. Alternatively you may try to cut higher up, though that is storing up a problem as the taller grass left then regrows faster. Basically a cylinder mower is for bowling greens, golfing and sports ground swards, and only any use when used frequently at short intervals.

Mowing less often = longer grass = harder to cut = which makes more bulk to carry away each time, and then the longer leaves left will grow back faster. Thus the sensible plan is to cut every five days or at least weekly during the spring into summer rush, though you can leave it further apart in droughts in summer. (When you move over to lightly trimming hedges, climbers and shrubs.)

Folk often expected to pay less per hour if you used their machines even though they'd also often expect you to get the petrol! The danger was that damage even wear and tear could become a contentious cost, yet it remained their machine. However I did end up with a few customers where I used their mowers as in most cases these were beautifully maintained, and their lawns were long standing and rather lovely to be cutting.

One was a retired naval officer. His garden shed was immaculate, the mower always ready, oiled and blades sharpened precisely. He was pleased to see it used often rather than for his sward to dare to rise anywhere above close cropped or crew cut as he called it. His soil was one of the heaviest clays I've ever had to dig, however this grew a lovely sward, and beds of excellent roses which were his pleasure and domain.

At the other extreme was a retired bank manager's sandy soil and impoverished sward. A powdery sand with some fine silt this lawn threatened to brown out any dry period of a few days or more unless it was watered. I find watering wasteful, but nice work, and it was needed here as the large unencumbered lawn had once been several smaller ones with flower beds set between them. To save time and the cost of a proper job laying turf these had been filled in and sown over, so their ghosts lingered on. The richer soil and stronger grass varieties made these green islands in the light green come khaki beige of the rest of the expanse. Thus to keep some balance I fed and watered the original part of sward far more, after almost every mowing of course.

He had one of the finest mowers I've ever used, it was built like military machinery to do the job ruthlessly and not to just look the part. This Shanks Dragonfly was engineering of the old sort, apparently easy to start I never needed to find out as he would bring this already running out of his garage and up the drive to me, full of fuel and oiled to perfection. What a dream purring up and down the long passes of his lawn while swallows would skim past. I believe this mower once had a trailing seat now lost but I walked, well trotted, behind as it clipped over the turf leaving it as beautifully finely trimmed as any bowling green or tennis court.

On the other hand with a rotary bladed mower powered by a powerful petrol engine you can cope with damn rough stuff, it may choke up but with persistence you can reduce waist high vegetation to chaff (and probably need new blades). But it is noisy rough tough work. Using a rotary to cut grass neatly is possible though never so fine as with a cylinder mower. Cutting is always less of a problem if the blades are sharp, and you collect the clippings. Some mowers have a back roller to give a stripe effect to the cut grass which a rotary does not make in the same way as a cylinder, even so it is still noisy and rough tough work, and also tougher on the grass.

It's because a rotary blade tears using simple impact force to smash the grass tips off. A cylinder blade is a continual pair of scissors slicing so smoothly their final effect is much neater. Plus by comparison though a cylinder mower will likely be petrol driven like the rotary but it will purr along almost quietly. Like well oiled clockwork it serenely tugs you along with the clippings flying in an arc into the box in front. It is so different an experience, and that final finish so much finer. But a rotary mower works in adverse conditions so is almost obligatory.

Although with inclement weather some days there was naturally pressure to get round to maintain the most urgently overdue gardens. But, once you were there and started grass cutting you could do no more than calm down and follow the mower. Doing all the awkward bits, corners and edges first then proceeding on to the main part. Relaxing in the inevitable number of passes up and down, the number of hods to empty. Up and down, up and down, stop, empty hod, restart, up and down, up and down, stop, empty hod, restart, up and down.

Monotonous to some however outdoors in lovely surroundings, and it's not always that hard work. Just takes time, and more when the grass is longer or wet. And so pleasing afterwards, a bit like painting, the pattern of stripes, the smooth billiard table green, and of course that distinctive unforgettable smell of new mown grass.

Make work designs

As with so many areas landscape gardening is rife with good and bad practitioners. But a huge mistake is to think a large company with plausible advertising is going to serve you any better than a small professional. Far from it, the bigger they are too often the worse their service. A man retired to a country farmhouse not far from me, knowing little of gardening he wisely decided to ask a large landscaping company to draw up plans with a view to having them make it over for him to enjoy and maintain. Partway in he rang and asked me to come and interpret the plans they had drawn up as he was really not sure they looked anything like what he'd wanted.

I drove over to his traditional Norfolk farmhouse set in a nicely large plot mostly all down to fairly tidy grass sward. This though not exactly level was at least obviously proving regularly mow-able. It looked like it would be quite an easy task to make over as there was so little to have to remove or work around, not even that many trees, paths or outbuildings to consider, mostly turf, which is effectively the best blank canvas.

Over coffee I asked what he had said he had wanted, he explained he'd wanted to have a bit more colour for anyone arriving, some fruit trees and maybe a small herb bed for the culinary essentials. He then produced the design he'd been sold. Unbelievable. Now I maintained gardens, it's often not the area of grass to be mown that takes the time to maintain it's cutting the awkward bits, narrow paths and tight corners. PLUS the keeping neat of the damn lawn edges to beds and borders. This plan had an incredible number of beds, borders and islands, each separated by a wee grass path, adding up to near half a mile of edges, all would be needing to be trimmed weekly or maybe fortnightly at a push. To say little of the sheer area of bare soil to keep hoed, and the vast number of plants they'd planned to fill up all those beds, borders and islands. I estimated it would take me one possibly nearly two days a week to keep these tidied with the weeding, grass sward and edges all to be done, as opposed to about an hour or two it took with a mower currently. He was so relieved, he'd thought it was just his lack of gardening knowledge that had made their expensive plan look fantastical.

I offered him my alternative, which was keeping it all down to grass with but two beds, either side of the front door backing onto the house wall so only a front edge to trim, a selection of trees and a small orchard- all on shoulder height trunks so they'd be easy to mow around, and by the kitchen door a raised planter in the sun for herbs. He was much more contented with this simpler plan, it cost a fraction of the other to install, and it takes him less than a morning's work a week to keep on top of.

Boules to that

Sadly as in any profession there are these Landscape Gardeners more concerned with selling a plan or truck full of plants than taking pains to find out what the client will most enjoy. They could spend more time asking them for their wants and needs rather than dumping a stock design on them, but with a company too often time and profit come first.

In one case I was asked for my thoughts on a design installed in a long thin garden stretching back behind a terraced house. This 'plan' had cost them a pretty packet yet seemed to have little actual design as such. Concrete slab patio by the back door with a small border running round, then a scrap of lawn becoming effectively a grass path set between two narrow borders running along in front of the fences on either side. It was uninspired, not low maintenance with a rubbishy selection of plants and a lot of edging. Most ridiculous was there was no provision for somewhere to house the necessary lawnmower which lurked at the far end under a plastic sheet, hardly an enticing feature to gaze towards. The borders had become weedy and disheveled within months with creeping weeds continually coming through the fences (to be fair there had been apparently total lack of weeding effort since the garden had been finished and handed over). On enquiry turns out all they had wanted was a garden they could sit in and they really had not wanted to mow, sow, hoe, weed, plant, water, tend etcetera any more than absolutely necessary. They would be prepared to pay for a prune and tidy a couple of times a year but that was about all the input this garden was going to get.

I discovered they loved holidaying in rural France, this gave me a solution. The borders and grass were removed, replaced with hard packed sand and fine gravel, a membrane along the fence line suppressing any weeds trying to get in. We set 7foot/2metre tall posts with wires overhead running the length of the garden and clothed these with reliable grapevines (Siegerrebe and Boskoop Glory). Where there was a bit more width near the fences a row of asparagus crowns were fitted in emerging through the sandy gravelly mulch. The cramped concrete slab patio area was extended to cover over the ridiculous narrow border so becoming comfortably wide enough for a table and seating area by the house. Best of all out from this extended the hard packed sandy gravel down the garden making them a perfect Boules Court under their vines. They were ecstatic, they soon made this an excuse and took another couple of trips to France to find Boules paraphernalia (posters, ashtrays, burnt Gaulloise and Gitane cigarette butts etcetera) to furnish their new court with authenticity. Meanwhile I gained a convenient contract for the maintenance, which was but some vine pruning, asparagus tidying and a tad of weed control with a sharp hoe, not too often.

growing like Topsy
One of the difficulties in maintaining gardens is that you have to work within the design, or rather lack of it, of the garden the client has inherited or bought into. Along with this randomness is the pernicious fact that ever since the time of the 'Great Houses' any gardens that have actually been designed have never ever been designed to make life easier for the gardeners who are looking after them.

Gardens if designed were predominantly made to look appropriate, or proper to the style then in favour. It was their primary rationale, aiming for that 'Chelsea Flower Show' appearance. Likewise designs for productive gardens were dictated by the requirements of the crops with not much, indeed very little consideration, to the well-being of their workforce.

It is attributed to, as I noted earlier, Gertrude Jekyll, to have the bizarre plan of small patches of bowling green sward atop fat pillars to be looked out on from upstairs and somehow bringing the distant lawn closer. Can you imagine the under-gardeners' language from on top the ladders as they make, water, feed, and constantly trim to a fine sward these ridiculous patches of sward a dozen feet up in the air...

Fashions, trends, merchandise to pump and dump, are not

new inventions but were well established business plans by the mid-nineteenth century when mass markets for gardening designs, for the latest plants and newest products evolved. With deliberate advertising promotion, books, newspapers, magazines and eventually television all ensure the 'right' sort / 'proper' garden' of the day will be dutifully emulated, interpreted, sold and miscopied myriad times. Then this amalgam as originally conceived has been altered over the decades as each garden passes down through the years with new owners.

Thus many of our gardens of today contain unique mixtures of elements surviving in a haphazard selection from proud owners long gone and 'lived with' ever since. Most probably your front hedge, gate and path are at least as old as your home, possibly pre-dating it. Few trees live more than a century but odd clumps of bulbs may be older still, maybe even centuries. And weeds such as bindweed and equisetum have likely been prospering wherever they are right now almost continuously since the last Ice age melted away.

Within each garden we find a somewhat random choice of plants. In some areas a keen nursery or garden centre can have influenced the additions to many gardens, but generally it's serendipity at work. There's also a tendency for certain plants to predominate in nearby gardens when these are invasive but still 'pretty' enough to be allowed; pot marigolds, false valerian and golden feverfew for example.

And of course there is the deceitful desire of some perfidious gardeners to donate wheelbarrow loads of their own horrors to unwitting novices. Others may inveigle them to buy pots of invasive specimens on some local charity stall thus infesting their gardens with seriously problematical plants before they've barely started.

Then the garden often evolves somewhat erratic plant positioning, often this where the owner has attempted to improve the display in a bed or border by impulse purchasing some plants. There is a great likelihood the 'convenient method' of arrangement will be employed. The first or biggest plant, as it arrives (not as it will become) will go in the largest gap available, the next to arrive or next biggest goes in the next gap and so on. A little thought will construe where this leads.

Now I'm not railing against any of this only exploring how so many of our smaller private individual gardens have become as they are. Seldom was there any actual plan in action except initially or where you are arriving after a sudden death or illness has incapacitated a keen designer and gardener. Most of our gardens have been continuously re-moulded with the whims and necessities of changes over many decades. Thus most are not very simple to maintain as little or no effort has ever been put into thinking through the regular maintenance requirements. Or sadly where they have been made over it is with a 'supermarket car park' mentality where as much as possible is filled with low-growing evergreen shrubs, not so much wrong as just disappointing though admittedly relatively little work.

So nearly each and every garden you come across could be improved to look better for less effort with a little pragmatic rationalisation.

Firstly, the typical larger garden will have some lawn and likely grass paths. These take a large percentage of the regular maintenance time whether done by the owner or visiting gardener. And each can usually be modified to save much of that time and effort required.

A lawn and grass paths needs mowing most weeks and edging fortnightly or monthly through nine of the twelve months. That's thirty to forty times. Because of this repetition if each mowing can be reduced by just a few minutes each visit then in a year that all adds up to hours saved, as also do the savings on fuel. Importantly, emptying the hods takes much of the mowing time so arranging either places to use the clippings or well placed wheelbarrows and receptacles can reduce this hard work significantly. (Clippings make excellent mulch if applied regularly in thin layers not in thick mats which go putrid.)

Cutting corners, it's inevitable
Often making small design changes, such as rounding off

awkward hard to get into corners, can save much regularly wasted effort with a lawnmower. Particularly annoying is where a section of 'lawn' fills an area between a tight bend in a path or two paths meet. Invariably folk will walk across any such corner making the grass bald and muddy so never looking nice yet still requiring mowing. If made into a bed they'll still trample across if they can. So legitimise their shortcut across the bend or angle with stepping stones, slabs, or alternatively just be mean and make the offending part a bed for spiky thorny specimens such as holly, pyracantha, yucca or gorse...

In one garden I maintained they'd inherited a meandering grassy path through large shrub borders to a leaf-mould bin living at the far end in an alcove. This long path was making wasted work when lawn mowing as the width was taking three passes with their mower, which had to get back out again re-mowing a wasted pass. Simply making the path a tad narrower reduced the cutting trips to one each way and still left plenty of room to push a wheelbarrow of leaves.

Whenever a lawn sits in the middle of beds or whatever then a modest reduction of removing a strip of say a foot or a third of a metre wide all round can save a significant amount in total. Of course in exchange you make abutting beds and borders correspondingly larger and needing weeding, however the soil revealed under a turf sward is usually fairy clean and easy to blend in.

Then more can be gained amalgamating two or more small beds into a larger one eliminating the turf sward running between them. This can save much of the mowing time and even more edging time. It's often worth simply replacing small grass path 'bridges' with a few stepping stones or slabs.

Always try making the whole area more convenient to cut; straight lines over any distance require little effort to mow, while a wibbly wobbly serpentine or scalloped edge to a border makes mowing irksome, really slow and risks back injury with all the heaving.

But by far the worst consumer of time for neat lawns and tidy grass paths was not the actual mowing but the edging as I've noted. In many folks eyes they need to see a bowling green sward, inset with sunken beds cut into the turf each with cliff like edges. Keeping those edges neat where they abut bare soil, mulch or whatever in the beds and borders is a hugely repetitive task demanding many hours over the year. The same rationale of amalgamating small beds into larger ones that eliminates a percentage of the mowing is even more successful at reducing the amount of edging regularly required.

many a mickle
I was asked to advise a small herb nursery that was finding it took them too much time maintaining their display area.

Indeed this small outfit was not keeping up with their actual production because they were spending all their time keeping their show garden looking good enough for visiting customers. This comprised a large collection of parent plants for cuttings and many other beds each dedicated to their many herbs grown from seed. It was all ordered, labelled, so neat, tidy, and insanely impractical. A lattice of small rectangular beds devoted to each and every type of herb were set in a paddock sized grid-iron of well mown sward path. Each bed of herbs separated from its neighbours all round with neatly trimmed and edged turf looked most appealing. However there were so many of them, a library of neat beds, worthy of a learned institution. The actual mowing of the grass was straightforward, up and down, and back and forth, quite a lot of turf would be gone over twice but at least it was all in straight passes. But those edges, those added up rapidly, small beds a couple of foot wide and twice as long have twelve feet or four yards of edge each! Think about it, each and every bed had four yards of edging to be kept trimmed! This was where all their time was going. Of course the edging could be mechanised, there are machines for the purpose, or, with risks of stones and debris getting flung about, the edges can be strimmed back with a nylon line trimmer. Either would still be laborious though, especially slow because each bed had four neat internal corners to keep pristine, rounding these into oval beds could save somewhat on the edging but would make the mowing slower.

I suggested replacing the whole internal lattice of paths with inexpensive slab paths set on sand. True this was expensive in time and cash initially, truck loads of slabs had to be laid. Though this was offset as their fine turf was readily sold, indeed I had even managed to sell it before it was lifted. However maintenance time was successfully slashed with only the surrounding grassed area left needing mowing, and with no more edging to do at all.

Another advantage was that by eliminating grassed paths from within the lattice work of beds the weeding time for the beds themselves was also much reduced as fewer weed seeds were spread about. This was further improved by sealing most beds under thick gravel or composted bark mulches, neatly retained in place by the slab paths.

raking bad
Of course in consequence of reducing an area of turf cut and edged you are going to increase the area of beds and borders to be kept neat and weed free. This can become onerous so is sensibly reduced by mulching. However as I say elsewhere unless you have perfidious creeping weeds or an appalling weeding regime then when wanted a neat bare soil can be kept weed free and tidy with a weekly or fortnightly hoeing, and then raking. Many omit the raking but it is THE finishing touch to an area of bare soil, mulch or gravel path. (Despite some foolish assertions it is

seldom a good idea to leave hoed off weeds as a 'surface mulch'. These never look good and if the weather turns wetter they may re-root or seed, worse they give off allelopathic chemicals that can harm our plants.)

Mulches benefit from a surface raking and whenever finishing off in a garden it is the point of perfection to brush down concrete and hard standing, patios and paths and then rake gravel paths last of all. This removes leaf litter, disturbs weed seedlings, redistributes the gravel, and most importantly, gives clients a great deal of perceived value for very little extra effort.

swapping sides
One of the hardest things to persuade clients was to take the longer term view rather than demanding a quick result or worse, an instant one. As I always quip "you can have a quick job, a cheap job or a proper job, even two out of three but not all of them together." Time is partly exchangeable with cost but is best taken slowly, in gardens planning over five or six years can give far better outcomes for less actual work and often less expensively than rushed jobs.

One customer had a standard conventional garden layout with a lawn in the middle flanked by borders on either side and at the far end. These borders were well planted with herbaceous and a few compact shrubbier specimens, a selection of good varieties, all nicely filling the borders back to the surrounding fence. Under which fence from all sides was coming, well rampaging, ground elder and stinging nettles, infesting themselves almost inextricably amongst the rightful inhabitants.

In one place the client had tried making a barrier with a slit trench and membrane (plastic sheet) but had not made it deep enough plus where it was in the light it looked awful as it degraded, then once brittle the weeds romped through it. Then they'd also failed to eliminate the weeds which had resurged from bits surviving each of their treatments. They'd tried mulching them out, then in desperation hand applying weed-killers losing some of their precious plants in the process. The problem seemed insoluble, or rather a lifetime of continual arduous hand weeding. (Looking on the bright side philosophically if you continually pull up then compost weeds growing under your fences in only a few decades you will have stolen away a huge amount of your neighbouring gardens' fertility.)

The solution is a simple swap, turn the layout around. In autumn I made one large island bed in the middle of their lawn carefully stacking the turf then digging over the relatively clean soil underneath. Few weeds even creeping ones extend far out under a lawn as the regular mowing dissuades them, but naturally there's tree roots etcetera to be evicted near the perimeter. Then the choicest shrubs were trimmed, lifted, their roots cleaned of all weed ones and planted in the new bed. Likewise the best herbaceous clumps were lifted, split, cleaned and replanted in groups of three or five. With all the more desirable plants transferred out those left in the borders were reduced to trash with a rotary mowing and covered with imported soil. Not quite to the brim though as these borders were then covered with the grass turves removed earlier. This turf soon established and the regular mowing then eliminated or at least suppressed anything trying to come up through the turf, including any more weeds arriving from under the fence.

We could have stopped there however the customers always right and they liked their old layout. So after a couple more years we dug a trench all round the perimeter, nearly three foot / metre deep and lined this with long lasting heavy duty plastic sheet which came well above ground (hidden from light and disguised being attached behind 'gravel boards' along the bottom of the fence). The old borders still had a few weed roots running under the turf but few by comparison with before, so the process was reversed. The turf was lifted and stacked (and weed roots pulled out of course) the soil dug over with those residual roots removed and the now well filled out plants moved back again, well spaced and well mulched. The turf was re-laid in the middle remaking the lawn and all became beautiful, with a tremendously reduced amount of work required to keep weeded.

hand weeding for ever
Naturally it's your garden you have the choice but a simple swap and remake can do the job as just suggested. However it does take long term planning and was refused by one client where it would have worked perfectly, and ironically would have been less lucrative for myself.

She had moved into their family home with a fine garden planned, made and maintained by her now recently deceased grandfather. In particular she loved a large, well massive, island bed of herbaceous plants. To be blunt this was no longer the vision of her childhood, not only over-run with ground elder and annual weeds but well in need of a re-work, splitting and replanting. Thus making a new near identical bed in the very large lawn next to the old bed was a most reasonable plan, simple and straightforward. But she wanted the old bed where it was. So a swap, improve then swap back suggestion was recommended. But no, she wanted the old bed renovated with nothing changed from her grandfather's plan. (Unfortunately most herbaceous plants slowly become larger 'crowns' which hollow out as these 'die' in the middle while impinging on their neighbours, thus the lifting and splitting every few years makes such an improvement. But no, she wanted them left and worked around. I repeat the customer (as long as paying) is always right. So I started by laying cardboard sheets between surviving clumps and covering these with a very thick, ankle deep, layer of the least expensive mulch (which was many truck loads of spent mushroom compost). This suppressed most of the existing weeds forcing the vigorous ones to emerge mainly in amongst the clumps. These clumps were methodically hand weeded every week while any weed raising a leaf above the mulch had more mulch dumped on it as soon as spotted. It took me three years of regular paid employment before the customer realised I had worked myself redundant and took over herself.

Some time later I espied she had not been quite as methodical and regular so of course the weeds had reappeared. This then ensuring even more wasted work for the longer they were allowed to prosper between weeding efforts the harder they became to kill.

As with grass cutting, the longer the gap left between treatments the greater the effort needed to recover. Never ever leave weed leaves emerged into the light long enough to make another leaf, unless you really do want to be weeding forever.

Sold a lemon, then another
One day I got a call from yet another potential client who had moved up from London for a life out in the sticks in yet another old farmhouse surrounded by large lawns. Would I come and cut these for them as they were having difficulty. I could use their mower (ie they wanted to pay less), which I parried with "we'll see when I've had a look".

I drove over, looking for a farmhouse set amidst a great lawn. Their road was long and with but one farmhouse along that road, so found it easily enough, but lawn! Knee high and not predominantly grass either. Not only was it well over-grown but it was also nowhere near flat, indeed it was undulating with bumps, lumps, and hollows. I strongly suspected a series of farm outbuildings built with clay lump walls had slowly decomposed and been allowed to grass over. Out the back of the house was a little less hilly almost meadow like, though showing grass long enough for hay. Indeed all their 'lawns' were more in need of farm management, or a total reworking rather than just a simple mowing over.

We went into an old barn where they had their mower. They had been to a nearby town to a supplier of new and used mowers (one I would never have used). They said they had described what and how much they had to keep cut (inaccurately I suspect as they really did not understand what was required) and came away having bought the firm's finest recommendation.

This was a mammoth piece of antiquated machinery, it probably had been state of the art when new, which was a long time past, indeed from before one and probably two world wars. It was dark green, circular, big enough to be a hovercraft, which it almost seemed as it sat on legs with oversized supermarket-trolley castors sticking out from under a heavy canvas skirt running all the way around.

This behemoth was a rotary mower, it had one single immense blade like a gigantic propeller a couple of yards across powered by an ancient oily motor also worthy of a biplane. This piece of kit was never intended for cutting 'lawns' especially not rough ones, it was made to trim a fraction of an inch off a cricket ground or football pitch where it would mow field length swathes six foot across. It could never ever cope with anything less perfectly flat, and certainly not be steered easily other than in a straight line. It was manifestly not suitable to be driven over an up and down, bumpy, lumpy sward with any degree of safety. And it would be totally and completely unable to chew through over-grown knee high grass and assorted field weeds. Indeed it had a somewhat limited choice of height of settings to cut at: close, very close, too close and standard (far too close), these so typical of most sward mismanagement in the past and particularly of sports grounds.

Despite its obvious dangers I had to try this machine out, it was like winning a ride on a classic steam engine or racing Bentley. The motor was surprisingly got going without much difficulty, though hugely noisy, smoky and not running smoothly but fitfully, the clutch was fierce, and with the massive blade spinning furiously I lurched forward. The speed it made across the ground was frightening as it bucked and shook. Perhaps this machine was perfect for a multi-acre flat as a billiard table sports ground but it was not suitable for this uneven surface, it was tipping and jerking about insanely, threatening to turn over. This was becoming too dangerous for me (which was pretty dangerous indeed as I was young and foolish) to continue. Their titanic machine was put back in the barn. I politely declined their offer of mowing with their machine, or mine, it was too far to travel (as well as too hard work and unprofitable). Perhaps they could trade the big machine for something more practical they could use? I advised what they needed was a rotary bladed petrol mower with an 18 or 20 inch or maybe 2ft blade at most and not that 6ft juggernaut.

A couple of weeks later they phoned me again. It was still not working out, reluctantly I went over. They had returned to the dealer and persuaded him to trade back the beast, at a loss of course. They were sold a replacement, though this turned out to be not quite what I'd described. They now had a new mover, true this was petrol and would cut a swathe 18inches wide, but it was as inappropriate as the prior one. It was a good brand but a cylinder mower not a rotary. As I noted earlier a cylinder mower can only cope with short grass cut frequently, it cannot cut back stuff that has over grown, even grass a few inches high is un-chewable. This was likewise unsuitable for anything other than a cut weekly nearly flat as a bowling green sward.

I explained again, carefully and slowly, then demonstrated

what they were after with my rotary mower I'd thoughtfully loaded up before coming over. Feeling sure they now knew what they needed I gave them the number of a more reliable dealer and beat a retreat. In retrospect I should have simply sold them my own mower on the spot for a massive profit. Even considered doing so, but spurned the opportunity fearing I'd be making too many return trips to keep it going as I suspected their combined mechanical skills would be at least as scintillating as their horticultural.

A moment's thought
An appalling case of paying for the proper job but getting a thoughtless mishmash was a client with a young family, and a new swimming pool, who consulted me over another case of plans not matching expectations. They had invested in an expensive concrete tiled swimming pool. This was, as often done, set half sunk in the ground surrounded by the mound of soil removed from the hole. No problem, indeed makes the pipework and pumps easier for fitting and access. However the client had then employed a well known landscaping company to 'make-over' the part of his garden this pool stood in. Rather than simply grass the sides of the mound with turf they filled that area, and some large island beds, with plants, at £x+ per square yard of course. Not an awfully wise decision for the sides of a mound as unless and until the plants form a mat over the surface they cannot hold the soil from

washing down the slope.

Now that was neither here nor there, you pays your money, however my client was upset by the scrappy appearance of these plantings. So I went over and had a look, he was not so much wrong as impatient. In general the plants had plainly not been in position long enough, and had not been tended well if at all and so looked rather poor. However they would look much better, even spiffing, the next season when they would have had time to establish. But to be frank it was a dismal selection with no theme or cohesion, indeed it looked as if it was a collection of left-over stock, basically plants they'd got cheap and needed a sale for.

What shocked me though was the choice of the plants on either side of the steps which led up to the pool. These were already grown large enough to flop over the steps where they were getting snapped and trodden on. Brilliant design, these were Euphorbias, plants with brittle succulent stems full of virulent burning white sap that will blister skin and even blind. What a choice to put right where friends, family and children would be walking bare skinned in the sun. He was horrified, this shoddy bit of neglectful design could have resulted in a minor family tragedy with rushed trips to A&E. I believe he got a full refund when he threatened to go public.

Beware, never assume

Pricing is as noted one of the more difficult parts of any new contract, and I soon learnt to be diligent inspecting all the terrain closely before quoting. It was too easy to assume that the 'lawns' were mow-able if you looked from the path, till you discover they have three years growth tumbled over and grown through. Or worse, there are hidden bricks and concrete blocks, metal posts or wires randomly distributed under the topmost layer. Wire fencing, even toppled fence panels can disappear from sight to become lurking icebergs to your mower as you blithely cut. Once I drove one mower onto the end of a scaffolding pole lying concealed half buried. This stopped my engine dead, completely wrecking it as the whirling blade bit an inch and a quarter into the thick steel end!

But the most foolish near miss I ever came across was when cutting the grass frontage to a pub. There were floodlights sitting on the grass and fortunately I'd spotted these were not professionally mounted. Neither were the cables heavy duty and fitted as required, and sensible. And then horror, these cables had just been laid across the ground to the lights one day in time for an event and had then been left over a year or more becoming submerged in the rough sward. The ultimate sign of insanity was the cables were permanently live, the on off switches being fitted on the floodlights. If I had proceeded to cut the grass without spotting these cables I, or anyone else, would most likely have been electrocuted.

As would anyone trimming a hedge in another garden that had the electric cable to the tool shed running through the hedge all the way.

They say every workman doubts the sanity of the preceding... Listen if you're going to be cheapskate and bodge stuff or employ someone unqualified then do so with your gardening, with your plumbing, your decorating, but never ever with your electrics please.

Short sighted economy
As I just said I always used to say to clients "You can have a quick job, an inexpensive job or a proper job, I can even offer you any two of those three, but you just cannot have all of them together".

And time after time most folk would inevitably choose the least expensive quickest option, more than a little foolish as your garden will be around longer than your television or your car. When you plant trees and shrubs they are likely there for several decades. Why put up with the cheaper seedling or 'common' variety when the grafted hybrid or choice selection may flower or fruit more magnificently for each and every year throughout all those decades, and for not much more invested initially.

And not only do some folk scrimp on the quality of the plants, and the work involved, but they somehow seem to imagine if you're a gardener you do it for love and live on air and home grown gruel...

Problem is people, especially those with independent wealth or on a more than comfortable salary, have no idea of how much it costs to live, and more so, to run your own business, all year through. They often have a somewhat ludicrous concept of how much you need to earn per day, every day, just to keep from going bankrupt. These same folk who spend tens of thousands of pounds on a new kitchen or bathroom every few years can get surprisingly tight when it comes to spending far less money on their garden. Which after all is effectively another room of the house, and the one that is on view to everyone passing.

Perversely if the current appalling and unjustified rise in house prices continues then they stand to make more profit on their home than they earn during the time they own it. A good looking garden is not just something to be proud of. It's the first impression a potential buyer receives. A garden can sell or stop the sale of a house. It's appearance and apparent work-load may be changing the value by more than say a superb or ghastly kitchen or bathroom might. Folk will happily buy a house and change a bathroom or kitchen completely but can be 'scared' of taking on what to them looks like an unsuitable garden.

UK is not Australia
Now gardeners as I said should work for free as we enjoy

it...

One miserable woman asked me to come and give her a quote for cutting her lawn, fortnightly (not desirable as I've noted as that is harder work for half the money of weekly visits). I arranged to see her garden as she was near another client, and gave her a very good price for a weekly mow and trim, the same at twice as much for a fortnightly. She was appalled by my quote. She exclaimed "When I was in Australia my 'lawn-boy' worked for half that." I pointed out that presumably he would be mowing all year round, which was the case, whereas in the UK we can only cut grass at best from March to November. Was she going to pay me a retainer for the remaining months? Of course she was not...

Builders' creep

Another client had had me maintaining her garden for several years, cunningly or more thoughtlessly, practicing continual 'job creep'. As soon as I'd agreed to add even more gardening tasks in addition to the established multitude she'd then try and add a few more. I'd arrive to find a list of things to be done, in addition to the mowing, trimming, tidying, dead heading and so on already undertaken and which I was about to get on with.

Worse, so many of her wish list items were totally out of season or just impractical as she was not a gardener herself. She was even more annoying in that she would visit nurseries and plant fairs, buying whatever she fancied at whim. It would have been enough to bring those back and have me plant them in suitable positions. But no, she would dig tiny holes and ram these plants into almost random spots, often in places already full, even in places crammed full of stinging nettle roots or ground elder. I'd rescue those I could and move them to somewhere they might survive. Her lists of extra jobs would be mostly terse notes such as "encourage the Hibiscus", which I would comply with, sort of. I'd give it a can of water and feed saying "grow, grow, grow" and tick that off the list. Or it might be "prune the old apple orchard" a task that would have taken a week or two on its own…

Anyway, back to the point of this client's extreme parsimony. I was having a coffee with her cleaner and mentioned I was planning on asking for a higher weekly rate, to cover the continual additional work and extra time I was having to take. The cleaner laughed almost until her sides split, and said I'd better be more than a little lucky. She'd been working for this lady for twenty plus years and when finally after many attempts at negotiation a raise was reluctantly agreed to be possible; it then arrived as an additional amount (per morning, not per hour) of just enough to almost cover a second class postage stamp of the day.

Last straw
One client soon found himself without a gardener when

he tried to chisel the cost down too far. It was the last straw, he had been trouble from the start. I'd originally been maintaining the garden of a neighbour, who had recommended me to another who I gladly also took on. Then this guy asked me to take on his front and back lawns as well. Having quoted him a fair price he then haggled me further, on the point, true, which was three gardens next to each other would be favorable to my travelling time and expenses. I reluctantly agreed. However, as always, I'd quoted a price per week throughout the whole growing season. This balanced the awful weeks when it was wet and the grass grew high overnight with the lighter work during droughts when the grass grew less if much at all. Actually turf always needs regular mowing if you want it to stay fine or it soon deteriorates, tussock grasses get a hold and perennial weeds will proliferate then predominate.

He'd got a very good deal and was apparently satisfied with my work when halfway through the season he had the gall to walk over when I was mowing his neighbour to say not to bother coming to cut his lawns that day. I could save myself the effort "as the grass hasn't grown much so you don't need cut it this week". And of course he did not say that he then did not intend to pay for a cut that would now not be done, until I queried this. When to add further insult he said the following month I could miss the following two weeks cuts after the next one as he would be away on a cruise, but I was to make sure it was all spic and span for the week after that when he would be back. That is he expected to not pay me for three weeks mowing as though the grass grew he would not be seeing it and then I was to catch up for when he returned. In other words he wanted to welch on this week's bill, pay one, skip another two and then pay a standard price for what amounted to a recovery cut. Which meant I'd have to work more than thrice as hard to cut such well over-grown grass ready for his return, while not getting paid for those weeks while it grew taller. I protested explaining once again in simple terms how grass grew and how my mowing and billing worked and that I was not willing to give up so many weeks of earning to then work harder to get back on top of his sward for him. He seemed amazed that anyone, especially a lowly gardening 'boy' would dare refuse his demands. He was paying and would have me do what he wanted when he wanted i.. I explained politely that I was self employed and I set the terms and conditions. He got angry and abusive, spitting out that I should know my place... I stood there amazed at his display of prejudice and arrogance, so gave the traditional British two fingered salute and told him in the vernacular to 'go fornicate elsewhere'. (Which loud business discussion was witnessed by the client who I had been in the process of mowing for at the time, and who soon informed me she thought he was a right **** anyway.)

Over the fence...

There are even worse people out there. I was quietly enjoying a beautiful morning diligently hand weeding a large herbaceous border by a wide gravel drive backed by a wooden panel fence. Annoyingly when I'd arrived there'd been some dog droppings which I'd immediately scooped up and buried. I'd thought these had been deposited by some visiting stray pooch as there was no fence or hedge along the road side only fences dividing off neighbouring gardens. Anyway, I was down on my knees grubbing out some ground elder roots when a steaming fat turd appeared right in front of my face!

"What the ****." Instantaneously responding to what had just happened I grabbed the offending turd (remember I had weeding gloves on) leaped onto my wheelbarrow giving me sight over the fence -where a neighbour was standing directly underneath. So shouting with quite justified outrage I lobbed it back down at her! A direct hit was achieved, with torrential abuse, promises of returning husband's violence, and threats of legal action. To which I retorted "Make my day, see you in court, our local newspaper is just going to love this", ending up with "do you really want your husband, the whole village and half the county to know about your absolutely disgusting behaviour dumping your dogs disgusting droppings over your fence?"...

Later that day I related my saga to my client apologising

for having antagonised their neighbour by my reaction (I know, never apologise, look I needed the contract) which did not bother him one whit. Turned out he had noticed errant dog poo, so not the first time apparently, and like myself had assumed some stray was to blame. He was outraged as I was, but not surprised, apparently the lady was a rotten neighbour in a host of other ways, so this incident just added to his list of troubles from her and he was in turn apologetic to me for my discomfiture while on his property. A real gent.

More job creep
Another couple I gardened for were pleasant, courteous, in most things professional, and like some others left totally unrealistic lists of 'improvements they'd like me to do for their garden. It is amazing, somehow they'd expect you to be able to do all their regular maintenance then by skipping a coffee break you could 'just' fit in pruning a massive Wistaria, move a hedge or make a new bed full of roses 'over there under the Weeping Willow'.

Of course by negotiation extra jobs could always be done but you had to be so careful of that 'job creep', okay if you could come to a fair fee for the extra work, but of course there is always a client who will just try to get more for less. I usually arranged a price per weekly visit not by the hour worked as customers wanted to know what they were committing to. But then of course they'd try and add another 'small job' to be included in the weekly visit. It was difficult to be firm but essential to point out from the start that expecting extra jobs to be done would result in a larger bill. But they would still try.

Having made and planted a fruit cage for this couple I kind of imagined they were going to eat their berries as these ripened and / or they needed or froze some. They did neither, bizarrely expecting having planted, pruned and maintained their fruit bushes I would also be picking these for them. Apparently they'd even been annoyed I had not harvested them and placed them in their fridge for them. I wondered if they also expected the plumber who'd installed their shower would come round and soap their backs...

One of the unwritten rules of business is remember you do not get what you deserve but what you negotiate. Never sell yourself short, better ask too much and bargain down, it is near impossible to try any other way. You can reduce your charge to win some lucrative business but be careful not to go too far. Never desperately try and win a contract through cutting your margins so far to then later discover you've under-priced badly making the whole job onerous or worse, loss making.

So always, always, explain fully then insist, that extra jobs added on mean extra costs will be added on.

Best avoided niceties

Nicer in many ways but more insidious to your business and one to avoid is the apparently kindly "would you like a cup of tea / coffee?" and indeed how hospitable, with biscuits or cake as extra bait. Some may be hoping by buttering you up they can persuade you to do them a 'favour', ie more jobs to be done, 'inclusively' of course. However much sadder is that many clients for a garden maintenance business are necessarily old and lonely, frequently widows. You may be one of the few visitors they ever get and some are determined to milk your time. Thus if you foolishly allow them to sit you down in their kitchen, never risk the lounge, you will then be held subject to an interminably long conversation. This often concerning their loving offspring who loved them so much they've all emigrated to Canada or Australia. You are forced to politely sit there until you can make your escape and all the time the clock is ticking.

It is hard, but either establish initially that you will be including the time for coffee breaks in your charging or be prepared to lose many hours of unpaid listening time as an amateur counsellor.

And that can be a problem. It is not so much the very human desire to avoid a long boring time with someone's tedious reminiscences but those hours slipping away. There are good and bad days for cutting grass and hoeing, that is when it is dry. In the UK even in arid East Anglia there are weeks when it keeps showering and never dries out for days at a time. Then when it dries out the gardener has to catch up with all the lawns that need mowing, all the beds that need weeding and so on. It is hard enough to keep on top of your own plot but when you have several dozen lawns and associated gardens each week to get round then it becomes frantic, especially in wet summers. Wet summers make the grass grow faster and so lawns need more cutting more often taking longer with many more hods of clippings removing, and so of course it's harder to get round as many as in dry weeks. And wet weather means the weeds grow much more so more weed control is required. In dry summers weeds and the grass parch and barely grow. A sward does need mowing so clumps of tussock grasses don't get away and fast growing weeds do not prosper. However, as noted above, some clients quite casually think they can save money by laying off the gardener during those weeks (just as they 'give you a rest / unpaid holiday' over the winter months). Anyway not paying for mowing in droughts is a mean idea, best circumnavigated early on by generously applying fertiliser and heavily watering their lawns each time you visit to ensure their sward remains beautifully green and lush all summer...

There's often space above
Most gardens are small, too small for the owners' desires thus often over-planted and congested, and worse over-

looked so not private. One of the most frequent requests is how to block out either the sight of something ghastly or the sight line of someone nosey. Nearly always when allowed (you may not block the light to someone else's window) folk usually imagine planting a tree, sometimes sensibly a thin pencil like Juniper Skyrocket or columnar flowering cherry. Yes, but it will take several years to be tall enough to be effective. Far more rapid is to erect a pole or build a frame of timber and cover this with climbers such as honeysuckle, clematis or grapevines. (Sensibly never rambler roses or kiwis unless you want to lose everything under a vast impenetrable canopy.) Likewise to get a large amount of impact from a border erect a tall post with wires to run up annuals such as sweet peas, morning glory or canary creeper, or train climbing roses or a vine on. Indeed a small garden can become hugely more productive and more secluded simultaneously by erecting substantial poles at the corners supporting perimeter wires carrying a grapevine or several all round. In fact a small garden can become quite productive when the space above head height is filled with fruit.

All you need is a small hole
One small town garden I advised on was a tiny patch at the back with everything from the front door to the pavement paved over with utilitarian concrete slabs to provide off-road parking. The new owners did not have a

car, indeed had moved to town because they did not drive. They had bought the house because of where it was near to a friend and imagined the ugly front desert of slabs could be easily lifted, taken away and replaced with a pretty 'cottage' garden. Moving in and having got settled they got a quote from a local landscaping company for improving their frontage. They were shocked and distressed at the estimate, many times what they'd guessed. On recommendation of a mutual friend they asked my advice.

Of course their quote was excessive, always is, but this time it was not completely unjustified. From the start these folk had naively assumed the front area of slabs could be lifted, sold, and underneath would be lovely weed free soil into which everything would be planted. Unfortunately, just for once, the original translation of a front garden into a parking area had been done properly, really properly, and by professionals. They had levelled and cleared away all the topsoil, dug deeper and back-filled the whole area with graded layers of rubble each well packed down, finely levelled with a sand layer and then a cement one on which they embedded the slabs in place, beautifully grouted between with more cement. Right proper job it was, neat, tight and weed free, carefully laid with a slight fall to shed rain away from the house walls.

Ugly as hell, it had all the welcoming aesthetic of a civic

centre, just lacking some gross piece of 'art' in the middle, waste bins and a bench. It would be a slow time consuming job to remove, with the cement making the slabs difficult to re-use or sell so needing costly disposal. To say nothing of the sheer effort of then removing and disposing of the deep foundations of well packed rubble. (I wondered what it was they'd once planned on parking, it was built substantially enough to support a fully loaded truck of steel castings, even one dropped in on end.)

I back-of-the-envelope priced up the job for them in comparison, though no way did I want this with the hard work involved. Obviously neither had the other Landscapers, for having removed the hard standing the area would need as many truck loads of top soil bringing back in to fill it back up to level. After that it was a doddle. But expensive to get there, in the end I reckoned it would cost about the same as the other guys.

What did they, well she, want, he was just there to keep her happy and pay the bills. Seems they'd dreamed of a 'cottage' garden theme, flowers, roses round the door etcetera. But no actual thought out plan or design at all. Brilliant. Instead of fighting the concrete slabs we could just work with them. A layer of fine gravel would make the whole far less brutal immediately. Then we could separate the garden from the pavement with deep wooden troughs holding mixtures of bulbs, bedding and biennials for year round colour to give their cottage effect. This reinforced and repeated with another pair of the same troughs stood either side of the front door, well out from the wall to catch more light and leaving similar space around the door for an arch. This had to be covered in roses.

Now here we come to the awkward bit. Large tubs could simply have been used to grow the roses in but they wanted their arch to be unencumbered. They wanted roses on trellis all the way up and over, not from big tubs stood at the base. I explained it would be an expensive task to remove a couple of slabs, and their rubble underneath, to re-fill with soil and make planting holes big enough to plant pot grown or bare rooted specimens. But with a hired hammer drill (used to drill holes for bolts fixing the base of the arch) I could easily make fat drill holes right through down into the subsoil deep underneath. First soaking then filling these with loam based cutting and potting compost. Into which (in autumn) I firmly set foot /30cm long cuttings of their desired climbing rose, the lovely thornless Zephirine Drouhin, this to root in situ and train up over the arch.

The same could be done with almost any easy to root climber or shrub, grapevines or figs especially as they love such a situation, and you only need a drillable hole through which to push a cutting which will then root. The hole width will eventually strangle the swelling stems thus you need drill suitably larger, say cup sized holes for potentially larger stems of the more vigorous such as grapes, kiwis, wisteria. However these more vigorous plants also have vigorous roots which could lift surrounding slabs so need careful consideration, possibly larger holes excavating, whereas the relatively puny climbing roses I'd rooted would not be likely to lift the surrounding slabs in this very well made parking area.

As is just said in this case climbing (NOT rambler) roses had suitably modest vigour so easily drilled holes were wide enough to let their stems swell over the years and still allow water to be poured in beside. The plants needed regular watering as the slabs shot all rain off entirely Remember any plant grown in any such 'patio' position will always need watering unless they are near enough to extend their roots out into damper soil beyond the edge.

Container survivors

One problem arising for a more modern jobbing gardener is the smaller gardens and the concomitant increase in popularity of planting in troughs, vases, planters and so on, all of which need regular watering. Whole gardens survive with virtually no attention when the plants are in the open ground. Even in droughts most may struggle through as their roots find the last drop. In any container the root system is much more limited, severely restricted by comparison, so the small amount of compost and plants dry out rapidly. (I say compost for it should be potting compost, ordinary soil does not serve well, it does not have the right texture or water holding capacity.)

When choosing a container do go for the largest you can manage, the volume is proportionately much greater holding much more compost to hold more water so lasting longer between watering. (And pragmatically if depressingly, larger heavy containers are considerably harder to steal away by opportunistic thieves.)

Anyway, jobbing gardeners are usually employed to come once a week as that fits grass cutting, and that is too long a gap between watering containers for most plants.

Most clients are willing to agree to regularly water their plants in containers, vases, window boxes which they have requested / insisted on, in between a gardeners' visits. Then in the real world they do not do so at all, or do so erratically which is nearly as poor a job. Then as plants fail and die many will claim it's the gardener's fault and not their neglect. Not a good plan for long lasting or comfortable employment.

So what can one do when clients want plants in containers in their gardens? Either insist on automatic watering being installed, or get paid for more visits on at least alternate days throughout the warmer months, or refuse to countenance anything in a container other than cactus...

Seriously, for an insistent client, the truly weekend gardener, for a holiday home, for that concreted over patio and where containers are inevitable, then only ever chose the very toughest survivors. Cordylines, pampas grass and yuccas endure neglect for amazing periods, oddly Christmas trees can survive unbelievably long times, as on the smaller scale may sedums, houseleeks and perennial herbs sage, rosemary, southernwood, ivy -and of course weeds.

It also helps to know the tricks for re-wetting dried out plants in containers as we all get faced with this sooner or later. Warm water wets faster, much faster, than cold, and a drop of washing up liquid increases the rate it's taken up even more. Problem then is often the top and bottom gets wet but the core stays bone dry. Sometimes standing in a saucer the water may be taken up, or the roots rot, but the middle still stays bone dry. Better solution is total immersion, I carried in my truck a plastic baby bath which was handy for this (and for mixing composts and small batches of cement and concrete) and which I still use in my greenhouse as needed. By standing plants in warm slightly 'soapy' water it's forced into every interstice soaking the compost thoroughly, after half an hour or so they then need removing and stood draining when they will be fully moistened right through.

Wrong way round
One garden I was asked to take on early in my career had been well planned and maintained by the owner who had now become unable to keep it up from arthritis. It was

helping him out that I realised how we often follow the advice without thinking through what the advice was intended to achieve. Two of this man's great pleasures were his bed of tea roses out the front and a gooseberry patch at the back. He loved a gourmet dish I also relish, a green gooseberry jam for which you need slightly under-ripe berries of varieties that do not ripen to red or the jam will also. Most of the rest of his garden had now been put down to grass though not these last two areas. He wanted me to take on the grass cutting, pruning his collection of roses as he had not managed for a year or two and to get rid of the weedy overgrown gooseberry patch. Then he remarked how ironically the roses had made a much better show since he hadn't been able to 'correctly' prune / slaughter them each autumn, and indeed were now suffering less disease, but were expanding over the drive and pavement. He wasn't happy about the gooseberry bushes, he had always sheared them over to keep them compact but untended they'd now grown into one unholy mattress of thorny shoots. Perhaps the only thing to do was to grub them out, he couldn't pick them anyway? But he loved their jam even though so many years in the past he had often lost most of his crop to mildew.

Listening to him it was obvious he had diligently 'followed' instructions but had never been a deeply thoughtful gardener just dutifully doing that as he had been taught was 'the right way'. Only thing was 'the right way' was right only if you were after the same result as the exponent of the method.

He had hard pruned roses as per the once obligatory rules, lots of precision as to the bud and angle of attack, and entirely ruthlessly, right down near to the ground. This method although adopted for general use was not originated to give a great show of roses to brighten the view but to produce a few huge blooms to win a rose show. By reducing all the top growth down to a few buds the root system was forced to make strong regrowth. This forced through a few buds made a few tall straight shoots topped with rose buds which swelled into massive flowers so heavy they needed wires to keep them up, and umbrellas to keep the rain off. All to win prizes. What most folk wanted was a show of roses. More blooms are got by leaving more buds = more shoots = more flowers. Simple really, but as there are more blooms they do not get as huge and so would not win prizes. And although the flowers are smaller there are so many more and over a longer period. A second advantage is when the bushes had been hard pruned the shoots coming from the few buds retained started low down near the ground so got splattered with mud and re-infected by fallen spores. When the bushes were no longer hard pruned every year the majority of the many buds retained were much higher above the ground so less infected by splashes. Then there was reason for his suffering less pests as well on the less pruned roses. When hard pruned roses (also as per instructions really well fed) regrow they do so through few shoots so the sap pressure in each is much higher than in myriad shoots from unpruned or sheared over bushes. The higher sap pressure attracts and supports more aphids which do not in fact 'suck' sap merely poking their 'drinking straw' proboscis into cells so sap pressure forces it through them.

He was amused, all his years of scrupulous hard pruning his roses had really been counter-productive. We agreed to just prune fairly hard initially to recover the bed then I'd lightly shear over the bushes each year after. That way he'd get a better display for longer. (And I'd not have to take away many bags of long thick thorny prunings but instead they'd be of spindly softer lightly thorned ones I'd risk composting.)

Then we turned to his gooseberry bed, these he'd grown just as had his father, as 'stools', deeply planted with many shoots coming out of the ground not all coming from a single stem or trunk like a tree. He had sheared these over annually to make space enough to get between and around each to pick them. With enforced neglect these had then grown into a spiny impenetrable mattress of thorns. It was obvious he did not want really to lose these either. Fortunately after a hard cutting back to induce regrowth these could also be recovered, and also made to crop better, more cleanly and more easily picked.

Indeed I explained if I now pruned them much more like he had been pruning his roses it would be better.

I explained by shearing the gooseberries over he had left a lot of buds which made many shoots with a large crop of many fruits which were then necessarily small. Then one reason they often suffered mildew was because they were congested with not enough airflow. Better prune more like the roses had been, cutting off most side-shoots leaving a sparse framework, with fewer new shoots springing into a much increased amount of vacated space. Thus less congested shoots, less fruits are set but each gets larger as fewer, easier to pick, and with less mildew as now the air circulation's much improved.

We had a good laugh, he hadn't been wrong either time just following advice not really intended for his purposes. He'd have had more of what he really wanted if he'd pruned his roses like he had his gooseberries and pruned his gooseberries more like he had his roses. Still, I would now do both of these for him, and pick the gooseberries which was now going to be a less prickly task, and with the bonus of receiving some jars of his home made jam.

An eye for rotters
As with most other itinerant work you have to be careful not to waste too much time and fuel travelling between gigs. Obviously, as noted, when you could get a cluster near each other this worked better. Well thanks to the

retiring gardener I mentioned earlier I had one local town cul de sac where I looked after almost every garden. I was hoeing in one front border when I noticed a van creeping up the road with a pair of occupants looking suspiciously intently over each property as they crawled passed. They went by not noticing me behind the hedge and continued to the end of the close turned round then returned, still crawling. Well they might be looking for someone, but they looked much more like they were scanning for places to rob. I stepped out onto the pavement taking my notebook from my pocket and in full view I wrote down their car registration number. They immediately drove up to me, stopped, got out and behaved in an aggressive intimidating manner.

"What the **** are you doing?"

I replied "Writing down your registration number, what's your problem?"

"We're looking for a friend."

"What's their name."

"John"

"John who? I know all these folk, I don't think there are any Johns in this close."

One got stroppy. "What are you asking for, why do you want to know, who the **** do you think you are?"

They were getting more intimidating, however I know the drill, show fear or even reasonableness and you're toast, you have to stand your ground and push back or be a push over. What is more they were not visibly armed whereas I was still holding my hoe. Now I'm no kung-fu expert but believe me I can wield my hoe both accurately, brutally, and persistently, after all I had had decades of practice. If they started any trouble they would probably be taken aback by just how nimbly I could give them bruised and bleeding shins and ankles, and all from a safe duelling distance.

I calmly looked straight at them.

"Look, I've got your number, so why don't you go somewhere else and if nothing happens here that's it. But any break-ins in this close and I'll be giving the Police your registration number with an excellent description of both of you and your vehicle. So go find somewhere else, please."

I thought they were about to have a go at me, they were obviously really angry at being confronted. Then, bizarrely one protested "Here's my mother's telephone number, ring her, she'll tell you I'm all-right and not a wrong 'un."

I laughed.

"Oh come on, there's not a mother in the world who would not claim her son was a good boy, have a nice day."

I carefully made a strategic withdrawal to inside the gate where I'd be better positioned if they made a rush at me. But they simply looked sheepish, got back in and drove off. To my great relief, it could have got nasty so easily and I had really not been wanting a set to. After all I was not paid to be a security guard.

Yes sir, no sir, three bags full sir, only way
Of course at other times concerned / nosey neighbours have called the Police about me, 'poking about next door'. Of course when the Police did ever turn up (and back then this could happen) it was obvious what I was actually doing. Mind you I did have to point out to one officer that if I was an opportunistic thief why was it he had caught me mowing the lawn...

Though it is essential to always treat Police with precautionary submission. I was driving home through the centre of Norwich one evening after a mammoth day. I had a lumbering great Volvo estate, the old sort you could slide a double wardrobe in (I had even moved a cast iron coal fired Rayburn range in this), with two roof racks on top each holding huge netted piles of rubbish bags full of leaves, twigs and grass cuttings. In the back of the estate were racks of tools along either side, a lawnmower jiggled in between, a nylon line trimmer, hedge trimmer and a blower piled on top. I was in green overalls and boots both densely bespattered with grass clippings.

I was annoyed being stopped by the Police for no obvious reason, but I calmly wound down the window and asked politely.

"Can I help you Officer?"

"Is this your car?"

"Yes sir" I replied

"Where are you going?"

"Back home near Diss sir"

"What do you do for a living?"

I was so taken aback by the futility of this question I foolishly blurted out "Brain surgeon".

Well that was stupid. I knew it. But too late.

I had failed the test, submit or be shat on.

They shat. My licence, M.O.T. and insurance papers were taken, queried, cross queried, checked up on. My car was then given an examination that would have done a prospective purchaser credit.

Now although old and never ever cleaned nothing could be found actually wrong with it, it was a Volvo after all. They then conferred, went behind together and tried to push it. For if it moved by even a jot they could then book me for having a faulty handbrake.

But these were not the forces' finest detectives. They were trying to push an ancient Volvo estate, the old sort, made from cast iron, granite and rolled steel joists with extra girders in the doors, fitted with a tow-bar and bumpers from a WWII tank transporter. This weighed more than most small trucks on it's own, plus, remember those two roof racks of compostable materials, all those hand tools, the mower, the power tools, the accessories, the fuel cans and kit, wellies and wet weather clothes, bottles, snacks and packs and all the detritus of working from your car. Even with the handbrake completely off it would not have been an easy push. Fortunately they could not budge it an inch.

Then one got mean, he looked at his watch and said

"It's gone lighting up time, and you are on the public highway without your lights on!"

I protested my lights had not been needed when they had stopped me some time before, but to no avail, they wrote out a ticket. The only ticket I ever received in more than fifty years of driving!

(Though more recently when near retirement I picked up another fine, this one for driving onto the expiring end of a newly created bus lane in Norwich ON A SUNDAY MORNING, passing through a camera positioned there presumably placed just to collect fines! I am especially exasperated by this as the whole raison d'etre given for excluding cars from bus lanes was in order to ease the buses' flow when traffic is heavy. This was early on a Sunday morning in mid winter when there were barely any dog walkers about let alone much other traffic! Indeed it may have been a bus lane but there were almost no buses about, indeed hardly any other cars about either. Fume, Fume. Okay, rant over.)

Poisonous intent, or Job's worth
Mind you that incident had been away in the great metropolis of Norwich, we seldom see buses round here so have no bus lanes. And the local police would not have stopped me, or at least I thought they would not as I imagined I was so well known in my area as a gardener. I had even tendered the contract for maintaining the Police station grounds.

But it turned out that my local police were not as alert and observant as I'd been led to believe when I had a most infuriating day concerning acquiring a Strychnine licence, or rather the Strychnine.

As anyone with a lawn in England (not in Ireland though) is aware we suffer moles. These come in hunting worms, grubs and so on which fall into their tunnels, which eventually collapse leaving hollowed depressions, and of course they make piles of soil that need removing (good stuff for adding to potting compost or borders though). I was not happy to kill them but would try if a client insisted. I found traps were effective but not time and cost efficient so were expensive a service to offer. These required too much time to set up and then required frequent regular inspections to ensure no animal was caught but not killed so needing humane dispatch to prevent their suffering. Gassing moles was antithetical to me for it would pollute the soil. The sole alternative (do not believe adverts for mole repellent plants, machines, devices, if they worked we would all know it by now) was Strychnine. This is a soluble scentless tasteless white powder extracted from a plant so it was 'natural' even though deadly. If a mammal eats the tiniest amount it paralyses their nervous system and they die painfully, though extremely rapidly. Worse, if another animal then eats part or whole of the dead mole it too will be poisoned. And awkwardly in the past people had not restricted using strychnine to poison moles and rats but had used it to solve other, shall we say relative, problems. So Strychnine was strictly controlled by law, very strictly.

But as this was the only 'natural' alternative I wondered how to get some, working my way through local and county councils, ministry leaflets and library reference books to discover first I needed to be granted a licence. I contacted the ministry headquarters in London, who passed me to someone who knew someone who would inform me how I could get a licence, if I filled in all the right forms, which they'd send, and then if I passed a personal oral examination. I agreed, gave my life history in triplicate and awaited their exam. This was conducted by a man from London who came all the way out to the sticks to inspect my lockable chemical store (old tin chest with padlock) in my secure premises (garden shed, with padlock), and my lockable chemical cabinet for transport in my car (old tin cashbox), and my protective equipment (same gear as usual plus face mask and rubber gloves). He then instructed and grilled me as to all the rules, method' and extreme care needed when using Strychnine.

This was informative and not at all unwelcome, he was genuinely helpful, though more than a tad condescending. I guess he was more used to dealing with less educated folk but he was so metro-centric. When he realised I was not moving my lips when I read a leaflet and could do simple maths he asked how I could live way out here in the countryside so far from culture? He loved theatre, especially opera and went several times a week. (I thought he must be earning well then!). I was so chuffed to smugly inform him my partner at the time was a professional coloratura soprano and that in our humble home we had a concert pitch tuned piano on which we duet-ed.

Anyway, I passed and a while later duly received a stamped, authorised, accredited, ministry licence to buy, possess and use Strychnine and with which I would be able to purchase mine from any major chemist.

I drove down to a larger nearby town with the illusion the job was as near done. The assistant balked at the licence and went to for the chief pharmacist. He came and looked at the licence, the sort of way cashiers look at your large denomination note, dubious, almost incredulous. He then said mere possession of this licence was not sufficient, he needed positive ID as he did not know me personally. And he then refused to accept my driver's licence, business card, membership cards, usual papers, cheque cards or even my bank statement of a local bank, saying to cover his backside he would have to see the licence approved ie appended with a validation of my ID by a suitable official.

"So who could validate this?"

He said the town Post Office manager would be perfect, it was open and nearby. I went and queued, eventually reaching the front to have a minion fob me off with some rigmarole the manager was busy and could not see me, anyway I should go to the Post Office in my own village".

Which they presumably knew only too well was run by a most correctly nit-picking-form-filling-box-ticking-do-it-by-the-book Postmistress. A pleasant lady, I knew her and her family well, as they knew mine, for she lived in direct line of sight of my front gate. I hesitated, she was so thorough about everything, you even feared she might demand sight of your passport before selling you stamps to foreign parts. I was worried, if the chemist was so concerned about getting this right, what would she spot, was my name clearly spelled clearly and precisely, the date, the address, was every detail provable in High Court. .

I returned home, had I a slow lunch and then went to ask her to sign the paper. (Tip- it's often good planning to ask someone for something in the hour or so after they have had lunch.) Which to my shock she did with surprisingly little cross questioning. Perhaps she thought better of testing someone about to possess quite a large quantity of extremely powerful instantly acting tasteless poison...

So I returned now armed to the chemist. He looked at the paper looked up and said he did not personally know this Postmistress so would not accept her validation. I swore under my breath.

"So whose would you accept?" I growled. He growled back "The Postmaster as I said earlier"

I pleaded he'd not been available. The chemist suggested I try again and failing that a Policeman. So back to the Post Office again, but the manager had now gone home not returning till the next day, and naturally the assistant was not qualified, so off to the Police Station.

Although a rural area this Police station was then defended by a number of security devices, doors and screens redolent of Northern Ireland. The story goes these were fitted after a fracas when a local farmer became convinced they were shielding a man who had been 'visiting' his wife. He had thrust his shotgun through the letterbox giving them all pause for thought. Thus the station had been upgraded to post-insurrection level. I negotiated to get through the door and up to the desk to explain my position showing the officer in charge my licence, which he perused for some time. He went to a cupboard and took down a massive tome, searching through he came to the designated list of rules and regulations. He then announced "a policeman was to sign 'that I was known to him as an honest and responsible citizen', and the problem was that he did not know me."

I asked for another officer who I knew did know me, for being a small country area my brother was dating and later married his daughter. Unfortunately he was away on holiday. Then I had a brainwave. I asked how long he'd been a constable here. "Five years." I explained how if he had been policing this small community for five years and he'd not heard nor come across me in some nefarious context then I must be an honest and responsible person. After all if he had just stopped me in my car would he not accept my driving licence as valid ID? Of course. Thus I must be me and he could sign. He refused.

I went back to the chemist. He still wanted a countersignature but I had had enough, I'd been farting around all day now. So I looked him straight in the eye and asked if he watched television, and did he know such and such show which featured a 'jobs worth of the week' where over-officious people were pilloried for their nit picking? I was about to go to the local newspaper and the television as I reckoned he had given me quite a run-around and I'd had enough, and anyway this could help me by being excellent publicity for my services.

He buckled, scrawled something illegible on the back of the licence, stamped it and went out the back returning with a paper bag containing two small bottles with skull and cross bones markings.

Ironically after all the effort and hassle to get the strychnine I never used it always managing to persuade my clients to let their moles live. It would have been handy if I'd kept it though, enough to wipe out the whole village if they annoyed me too much...

A near miss in Diss
I spurned most chemicals of course. I wanted to be as Organic in my business as in my own garden. However there was a difficulty with weed control, not in gardens but in the grounds and car parks of business and factory sites. In gardens it was simple enough to control most weeds with a sharp hoe used often, ground cover fabrics and mulches, or just putting it down to grass and mowing. But large areas of tarmac and concrete paths and parking can be destroyed by weeds within a couple of years if they're not stopped and are just not suited to control by

those methods.

I had come across flame guns, these were portable and produced a small intensely hot flame, they were not at all like WWII flamethrowers for their flame was much much smaller and stayed close to their nozzle. Their intensely hot blue flame was more like a Bunsen burner or gas hob. The idea was to pass this flame rapidly back and forth over weeds merely searing them. These would then wilt and shrivel weakening the plant leaving dried up remains to be burned off at the next visit together with any re-growth. A few deep rooted weeds might recover from a second or even from a third visit a week or two apart but one more treatment would always deal with those. And it was most effective on such difficult problems as graveled paths greening over with swathes of seedling weeds.

Now you need suitable clothing depending on the task, especially when using machinery, and a flame gun even the more. I wore quite a lot of ex-military gear, not from style but because it was tough, relatively un-inflammable, and inexpensive: leather flying gloves and excellent boots, Balaclava helmets (elasticated cover for entire head and neck, with face-hole, ideal for keeping flying rubbish off when hedging and so on), khaki camouflage overalls. One day I was all togged up having just finished with my flame-gun on a graveled parking lot when a chap who had been passing by paused to suggest I was a really brave, or very foolish man... So of course we got in conversation I imagining he thought my long metal tube with flame coming out the end was a fearsomely dangerous weapon. Far from it, turned out he was off duty military, had just returned from a tour abroad working with the same US A10 tank-buster flying gunships that frequently roared past low overhead practicing their WWIII tactics aiming at East Anglian farm tractors. He pointed out how these warplanes had infra red detectors that would 'see me' and compute my flame-gun's flame profile as very likely a ground-to-air missile being launched by some terrorist. Simultaneously their ground radar computer would identify the flame came from a tubular metal object held by a human. Now if I was very lucky the plane's automatic anti-missile missile system would be correctly disabled whilst over friendly territory... which would mean it was instead immediately alerting the gun happy pilot onto visual, where he would see someone in military garb wielding an already confirmed and definite threat...

He reckoned I was not far off from becoming a hole in the ground and an implausible public excuse waiting to happen. I got his drift, and was much less willing to get out this useful tool when those A10s were about. However I stopped for another, rather obvious reason, an open flame simply proved too risky a process, insurance was harder to get, and I had a bit of a, shall we say, mishap.

Burning disaster
Obviously I was sensible and would never use a flame-gun

under or even near a parked car, gas bottles, fuel store, or indeed anything at all flammable. But one afternoon I was using mine to clear a gravel drive of a flush of small seedlings. Slowly walking forwards, a step at a time, swinging the flame side to side so all the weedlings got first wilted then cooked. At some point an unexpected gust of wind blew a tiny glowing fragment of leaf away behind me unnoticed, and malevolently dropped this onto some parched dry grass and leaves under a towering conifer. I was unaware of the impending catastrophe as I continued working my way down the drive till my eye caught strange flickering reflections in a car window. I turned to see the tall coniferous tree burning like an upside down rocket with a rushing crackling roar. Too late to do anything but watch in panic. Luckily the clients were not attached to this tree and in fact had rather wanted to have it down, but it was an important lesson –reinforced when my insurance came for renewal.

Back to college

Sadly once the flame gun was discarded then the only economic way I could keep large areas of drives and parking lots clean the way the clients wanted was not Organic, it was herbicidal weed-killer. Still I would rather I was to use such stuff, really carefully, than let someone else with less principals throw it about. I hated to have to use the stuff but could see no alternative. To add more difficulty I would have to study at agricultural college and take an exam in pesticides usage if I wanted to use the stuff anyway as new legislation had been brought in controlling pesticides. (After some nasty accidents that were quietly hushed up.) This legislation had effectively been drawn up by the companies that produced the chemicals, apparently more for their convenience and profit than public safety, and then been ratified by the ministry.

The course I studied was all about how to apply the recommended (usually a maximum) amounts of highly toxic chemicals 'safely'. To remove any competition for their products it became illegal to use any thing not stamped with a ministry number (which of course could only be gained by an accredited chemical company). It also became a criminal offence to use, make, recommend or store anything else for use as a pesticide. Thus neither shaving soap nor Lux flakes were to be used or recommended anymore to kill aphids, and neither were Rhubarb nor Elderberry leaf teas. Even sticky tree bands and pepper dust were covered. Basically you couldn't apply anything other than a commercially sold approved product at an approved rate in an approved way in someone else's garden or on public land or you could be fined unless you had qualified with the necessary certificate to do these things.

Naturally I understood, even agreeing with, the raison d'etre of such legislation, it was just the degree of implementation that was so onerous. Seriously, Sodium bicarbonate as I learnt when cooking is Baking powder, the same stuff considered safe enough to put in cakes, this was made illegal and banned as not cleared for use as a fungicide, probably because it was a competitor that was remarkably inexpensive, too widely available and surprisingly effective.

Anyway, I attended the local agricultural college for the obligatory course, I did not mind going there in any case as I liked to use their library. Well, the sessions were not much about theory more about how to calculate with pen, paper and calculator, how much hazardous concentrate you would add to a given size tank of water on a tractor sprayer that would deliver so much per minute through nozzles on huge booms that would cover so many square metres. I'm good at maths, most folk are not, it was tedious, I could do the calculations with ease but was obliged to wait while others endured their laboured exercises till they near enough got it. It became apparent most if not all the information was not aimed at gardeners such as myself but more for agricultural workers applying all sorts of nasties to food crops by the tractor load.

Though I could understand why, it seemed bizarre I had to learn how I should fill a spray tank of a forty foot boomed tractor to apply the exactly correct number of milligrams per square metre when it was travelling at 8mph! But to be fair others griped even more, and with good reason as well, the council road sweeper who occasionally had to treat pavement cracks reckoned at least half the course was a total waste of his time. He was employed though and so had his fees and time paid. Many of us were self employed and of course this was not a free course or exam. The most upset were a couple of interior decorators, their only prospective 'crime' they could think of was they might have needed to deal with some pesticide residue coming off some office or houseplant material. Teaching them how to soak a ten acre field uniformly with something seriously dangerous from a tractor did seem a tad pointless. Especially as simply to avoid prospective lawsuits they had long decided they would never be using any chemicals anyway.

The Law is not always an ass

One curiously worrying bit of information was when we got to the 'what to do with old out of date or unlabelled pesticides'. We were told to dilute them down then spray them on paths, roadways and wasteland! Several of us protested and said we couldn't do that as we were gardeners not farmers and did not have that sort of vacant space. The answer was to call the council, who would arrange, at our cost, the safe collection and disposal of the chemicals. A man would turn up in a specially marked truck, put on the complete hazard protection suit, boots, gloves and breathing equipment then with long handled tongs carefully transfer the suspect items into a sealable crash proof flask and take it for disposal.

"What happens to it then?" we asked.

"It's disposed of in an authorised manner on a registered site."

Someone ad-libbed "I've heard he drives to a company lagoon near the coast where he lobs it in". This was not corrected.

Another ironical twist to this legislation was the grandfather clause, which kind of admitted in a way just how hazardous some pesticides were, and had been. There had been difficulties bringing in this new legislation as there were so many agricultural folk who with the change in law would now have to become qualified if they were to carry on working. It was realised there were two problems. The first was compliance, younger farmers would study and gain the qualification, but many older and especially very old and cantankerous farmers, were unlikely to comply, regardless of threats etc. Secondly sheer numbers meant if in fact all farmers and farm hands actually complied the trainers and examiners could never get enough of them through fast enough without there being serious queues and backlogs for far too long. Thus they invented the 'Grandfather' clause which amounted to 'If you have been using pesticides in your work and you have done so over long enough time when you have also become a grandfather (ie presumably you have not accidentally imbibed enough to wither your gonads away) then you may continue to do so without currently needing to come and be trained and qualified.'

Doesn't work anyway

An irony was that having now become qualified I could buy and apply chemicals not available to the general public and thus presumably more effective (and of course more risky). But chemicals effective on a field scale did not necessarily work in a garden situation. You see most weeds coming from seed in garden soil can be disposed of by a multitude of methods just as well as by herbicides. Even weeds recurring from a deep taproot succumb to similar treatments simply needing multiple passes. The difficulty comes with weeds with extensive root systems that then can only be killed if you can treat the whole system simultaneously. These seldom become a problem on a field scale because of the sheer size of the areas involved. But if you have, in order of invasiveness: Ground Elder, Japanese Knotweed, Bindweed or worst of all, Equisetum in your garden these will not only be in your garden but in all the gardens next door, and probably all the gardens in your street, even getting into cellars, attics, under floors and up inside walls as well. One plant can have a root system infesting many acres. As fast as you kill off the parts in your garden or allotment plot more encroach to replace them. Even an isolation trench may not work as some weed roots can dive down metres and come up again the other side of a street.

One factory site I looked after had Equisetum coming up everywhere, in the car park, access roads, even inside the buildings. I sprayed it with herbicides. Then I sprayed stronger stuff. Then I battered the foliage and sprayed that. Still it came back. I apologised to the client explaining the only way we could stop it was by spraying the neighbouring plots as well thus killing the whole plant at once. This was not going to happen / be paid for, so from then on I restricted myself to tidying off the foliage with a nylon line trimmer, there was no point doing more.

If however this had been a patch all within a field it could have been completely dealt with. I got rid of the much feared Japanese Knotweed from a garden where they had foolishly planted this attractive weed. It had formed a clump the size of a small bungalow, however most fortunately this was surrounded by lawn, only rough lawn but mowed often which was confining the plant to some degree. Chances are it would eventually have escaped but I was able to deal with it in time. First the top growth was cut to the ground in winter and burnt. Then a rough mower was used every week of the growing season cutting off every shoot before it could unfurl and recover the energy from sunlight to make another. A year later very few shoots were still appearing and regular cutting continued another year, and for the year after that when there were no more. The area was however kept down to cut grass thereafter just in case and to prevent seedlings springing up. Job done.

Foolish mistake

Now although qualified to use chemicals I'd always try and persuade clients there was no need for them. However if they insisted I'd rather if they were to be used that at least I as a qualified sensible person would do so not some fool who might do more harm. As with moles I usually succeeded in finding alternatives, but not always.

One couple had moved up from the city to an old farmhouse at the end of a very long track. If you are wondering why so many of my anecdotes concern such incomers' gardens it's because locals often did their own gardens (though many did not garden at all having other uses for their land such as keeping hens or collecting dead cars.) Anyway this long track was narrow and deeply ditched on either side, the daily traffic kept the wheel-tracks clear, with edges and down the centre scuffed to rough grass and prostrate plants such as daisies, marjoram and wild thyme. Beyond a foot or so either side the edges sloping down to the ditches were covered with all sorts of native undergrowth, mostly stinging nettles and brambles arching over the ditches. They wanted all this sprayed bare!

I protested, not just at the amount of time and quantity of chemicals required to kill off such a vast area of natural habitat but the sheer foolishness. I explained how the traffic kept the 'grassy bits' trimmed and that the banks of perennial weeds would look ghastly if killed with a spray. Worse, without the perennials filling the space then the bare soil would soon be covered with wind blown seed weeds which would then require spraying again and again.

They did not listen. I refused (well quoted so high an estimate they declined) to do so much unpalatable work so they paid a local lad (who was untrained and unprotected) to do the job for them. I was gratified a year or so later when they asked me over to do another, different job for them (laying a hedge, a job I relished as it's skillful, and warm work in winter). As I drove in I saw just as I had predicted that the entire length of the track was now a mass of dandelions, groundsel, thistles, willow herb and other more pernicious weeds. These wind blown seeds had come onto the empty soil left bare when the existing covering had been destroyed. Now these were flowering and billowing clouds of seeds were being pulled along the track by each car slipstream. These seeds were carried along rapidly converting the farmyards graveled turning circle, parking bays and courtyard gardens into an equally weedy mess. I think I may have been a bit smug with my "I told you so."

All in the dose
I was working in one garden when I noticed in a field entrance opposite there was a bare patch near the road

that nothing was growing on. I assumed this may have been where a pile of road salt had stood as that would do the trick. Talking with the owner turned out the burnt patch had been a burst bag of fertiliser, the farmer had shoveled up what he could but the remainder poisoned the soil, for a long time, even after it had been washed away diluted by the rains. People do not realise how any salt, and fertiliser is just another salt, can kill just as if it was herbicide. Put a teaspoon of salt or granular houseplant food onto a dandelion and it'll soon have all the moisture sucked out of it so that it then withers away.

Well I had a call to a lady on the outskirts of Norwich. This lady and her family had moved into their new home with a beautiful established garden the previous year and everything had been fine. Now her story sounded terrible, seemed some farmer had sprayed too close to them, or some pest or pathogen had got in and was now killing all her plants, everything was a disaster, she was distraught, desperate for advice. As I drove up to her house everything looked very wrong, Laurels along the drive had three foot long yellow shoots, more similarly deranged Lilacs greeted me as I arrived near the front door. A mixed border on either side was indeed looking like it had been sprayed with something, but so did almost everything else. I looked closely, each and every plant had an odd mulch of granular whitish stuff in a ring around it. Larger plants had even more of this strange mulch. I knocked and greeted the clients, turned out they were not gardeners at all but had taken on a large garden as it was 'ready made' so they thought they could cope. I enquired about the odd mulch. Seems they had inherited a stack of sacks of farm fertiliser in a shed and decided it should be applied, but had not worked out what sort of dose was sufficient and somehow they had imagined it was spread about the plants a bit like muck or manure. So each and every plant had got a share, not the tiny amount required but more than enough for several decades and all in one go. As Norfolk is a dry county only part of this toxic mulch had yet washed in, things would be worse when it did, probably even killing trees and hedges surrounding the garden as well as within by polluting the water table which was not far down.

Well as much as could be was carefully collected up. Scooped up with much of the soil it amounted to a dozen sacks, which I disposed of safely (okay so I sold this on to other clients feeding it to their lawns a small quantity at a time). The residue that could not be scooped up was hosed away so at least becoming well diluted. Some of the tougher woody perennials survived indeed even looking wonderfully lush for a while. Sadly it was too late for many of the softer, smaller, herbaceous plants which were lost, though a few that survived did get unusually large and went the most verdant deep mossy green. The moral really is you can have too much of a good thing.

Can't pay, no won't pay

As anyone running their own business will tell you it's not getting the work, nor doing the job, but it's the getting the money after the work has been done that is by far the hardest part. Not just the miserly approach most folk have to their gardeners but getting some of them to pay at all. There are a small number of not nice folk who are pleasant and friendly while they're getting you to take on the job but become remarkably absent and or absent minded when it comes to paying. They all use the same old ploys over and over again: Not had your bill, send another. Will pay you next week / next Thursday. Sorry misplaced my cheque book / run out of cheques. It's in the post. It must have been lost in the post, I'll send another now. On my way to a funeral, will call you when I get back...

The problem is once you've worked for them they owe you, you foolishly continue so then amounts add up, thus they get you hooked, the more that is owed the more you lose if you simply walk off. They know this so their approach is to pay initially, then after the first few payments you get nothing more until you threaten to quit or call a lawyer, then they'll hand over just enough to keep you working a bit longer. There is no solution to this as sooner or later they will probably stop payments altogether, and /or likely disappear. Or you get so fed up you remember the golden rule;

'the first loss is always the smaller loss'

and simply stop working for them and write their debt off to 'experience'. (And never ever after writing rude messages on their lawn with weed-killer...)

Naked truth

One property developer was restoring a grand house and prestigious garden, this was a plum job though incurring much travel and other costs. (Much later I was informed I probably only got the contract as most other contenders had already been bilked by this shyster.) Same pattern, first payments made though very slowly, then more delays, later and later, and part payments, even longer delays, excuses, more excuses then stonewalled. With such a huge restoration the work had to continue but I was reluctant to keep doing so for the glory alone. Eventually I went to his office, with he refusing to see me I refused to leave, and engaged every visitor with my tale of his financial unworthiness. They threatened to call the Police, I agreed, explaining I would strip off naked outside and make a story for the newspapers putting my case before the public, and all the folk in adjoining offices. It was a short pause then he sent a cheque out. As it was for the bulk of what I was owed I rushed at breakneck speed straight to the bank for immediate processing fearing it would soon be stopped. Having cleared and with the cash in my account I reckoned it would not be a clever idea to allow him to run his account up again. Loved the job, and the place, but needless to say I never did any work there again.

Insurance job

Another shabby couple had a car go through their garden fence and across their 'lawn'. It was agreed by the driver's insurance they'd pay so the couple hired me to repair the damage, and of course as everyone tries they wanted to get more done on the insurance than entitled. But by much more than the usually implausible degree. They wanted a Chelsea garden makeover when in fact almost all the damage had amounted to was a hole in an already old and knackered fence and a couple of ruts across their 'lawn'. I priced up a fair job for them, better than before but not excessively so, adding new gravel for a 'soiled' path and several 'replacement' shrubs which were not strictly necessary. They'd also wanted the job done in a hurry for a celebration. I was always eager to please and even finished laying the turf by my vehicles' headlights for them. I then asked for payment. You just know what is coming, most pay on the nail, there and then, and those that don't are going to be trouble. And this couple of shysters were trouble. All the usual excuses, doubled and repeated. It was all the insurance companies fault not theirs blah de blah de blah. As each day passed another excuse so I drove round early one morning and with a couple of mates noisily began lifting and loading the turf (this takes several weeks to root down firmly so re-lifting was not too difficult) back onto my trailer. They rushed out cursing and swearing at me. They tried to make out I was stealing their turf, to which I pointed out I'd stipulated, as always, that all materials remained my property until paid for. They threatened to call the Police, which I told them to do knowing full well the Rozzers would never intervene in what was manifestly a private business dispute over payment. The thoroughly nasty pair soon realised I was serious and after muttering between themselves agreed to give me a cheque- which I knew damn well they would be thinking they could stop before I could get it cleared. So I informed them they had better not stop the cheque or they'd find the turf gone again, and I would have them prosecuted for fraudulently obtaining a pecuniary advantage by deception, a criminal not a civil offence. Which had the right effect and they found the amount in cash surprisingly quickly.

Don't get me wrong, the majority of customers were fine, paid as agreed with seldom a query. Little old ladies with hardly a penny to spare were most prompt whereas predictably the apparently wealthier were meanest and tardiest to pay, and naturally theirs were also most often the larger bills.

As with building jobs there is the added complication of materials. Most customers want you to arrange it all with your supplying all the materials so once the work has been completed they can settle it all in one. But this exposes you to late payment, which then means you are running credit for them. And even a small landscaping job such as a patio is hundreds or thousands of pounds worth of materials, the interest alone is a serious cost. Worse, if they then don't pay you lose not just your time and efforts but risk all that cash invested in those materials. So upfront deposits are the only sensible way when any large amounts are involved, ideally with staged payments as work progresses, ie at any point you are only risking a small percentage of your cash in materials and work

REMEMBER- IF anyone ever agrees to your terms in any negotiation (which if you have any sense you should have started off with asking more than you dare) without them trying in the slightest to get you to charge less in some way or the other, then be wise to suspect they probably do not intend to ever pay up at all! Poor folk do not often part with their money without serious negotiation and trying to get a better deal, richer folk never do.

Word gets around
One small advantage of living in a rural area is you know so many of the other businesses. This saved me when a new customer I'd not dealt with before wanted me to quote for several lucrative jobs. It all sounded excellent, there were many improvements he wanted: patio, loggia,

fruit cage, mini orchard, it all amounted to weeks of work. I went home to price up the jobs, but smelt a rat, he was too glib. Now I'd noticed he already had a brand new fence which could not have been up for more than a couple of months, he'd said he'd moved into the house the autumn before so seemed likely he'd had that done. I rang round, did not take long as I'd recognised the distinctive workmanship of another gardening 'firm' (or perhaps it was their lack of workmanship...) and surprise surprise the fence's payment turned out to be in dispute. As with myself this firm had been promised loads of other business, the fence had been done first, then when the client stalled paying they wisely stopped and no more of the jobs were started. Seems he had also bilked a plumber, and run up bills for straw and feed. Some people with, shall we say, a short-sighted attitude move to the country and think they can behave as they had gotten away with in the big city, but word gets around fast in a small area. And he was careless, only a few months later his new shed supplied by someone less well informed burnt down one night not long after he'd locked his new mower in it. Must have been the engine was too hot to shut away in such a closed up space and some dried grass had caught...

These modern houses all look the same
Of course we all make mistakes, even the most careful. I had won a landscaping job for a new house on a new

estate. I turned up to this moonscape with houses, all was levelled mud with the buildings, rather close packed though each did have it's own small, muddy, fenced in plot. Obviously the estate was just finished so barely anyone had had time to move in, I could see many bare mud / garden plots awaiting attention, a lot of prospective business. Met up with the new customer, who wanted his new garden all down to grass as he could cope with that. A wise move for those who don't want a garden as such, small areas of grass are not a long nor hard weekend job with an electric mower. Indeed far more folk started cutting their own when Hover mowers were introduced as these could be brandished about more easily than all those that went before. Laying turf was not my preferred landscaping task and the material only gave a small profit margin compared to say filling a border with plants. Though it was still work, and as it could lead to more all round, it was worth taking on. So I measured up, quoted what was almost a loss leader price, which was agreed, a deposit taken and I went off to return the following week when I'd set aside a day for the job.

The day arrived, I loaded up and set off, drove into the estate early in the morning with a trailer of turf, and cunningly a wad of advertising flyers to put through all those prospective letterboxes. I parked and before I got muddy and sweaty walked up and around the whole new estate distributing my leaflets through the letterboxes or where there was none I tucked it neatly into the door of every new house, there were many new homes and almost every one needed a garden making, I sniffed a profitable period coming.

Then I had a coffee break (strong, very sweet, filtered ground Organic coffee from a Thermos flask I took with me as I never could stand the awful ersatz brews folks will serve you, which one, charitably, assumes they may even actually drink themselves). Sitting on the stack of rolls of turf, it really was a beautiful morning, sunny with a light breeze. Made all the better by the prospect of at least a couple of new garden contracts I might land, so I planned an especially neat job here as first example. And to make sure everyone going past knew it was my landscaping and how to contact me I'd brought and fixed my advertising board to the fence before I got going with anything else.

I was diligent, carefully forking over and removing various bits of detritus the builders had strewn randomly about then rammed into the ground all round. (I imagine this is some ancient ritual they feel obliged to re-enact). Then I dug over, raked and levelled the mud until it was flat enough to be acceptable. Finally laying the turf I went home happily tired after a full day. Called to tell the client the job was done, they looked forward to seeing it at the weekend when they came up, promising they'd water it as soon as they arrived.

Friday came round and I got a telephone call late in the evening to say what was I playing at, I said I'd done the job but they had no lawn!

"What?"

Had it been stolen? Possibly, freshly laid turf is easy to roll up and take away, and it's worth as much as expensive carpet. I rushed over to the new estate in the dark, slowly drove round, theirs was the only house with lights on. Stopped, got out, and they were right, no lawn, nor any signs of there ever having been one. They opened their front door and as I was about to go inside with them I turned back to lock my car. In the dim light I saw exactly opposite, in front of another identical new house, was an obviously freshly laid new lawn, one that looked remarkably and awfully familiar. And staring at me fixed on the fence around the lawn was my advertising board. Somehow that morning I'd gone widdershins before distributing the leaflets. I'd been so engrossed with the prospect of gaining more work I'd fixed my board to the fence outside a house on the *opposite side* of the road. From then on I was doomed, I'd obviously laid the turf in front of the wrong house on the other side of the road.

Thus I had to return to lift and move it over, to lay it again this time in the correct (and unfortunately needing as thorough preparation) garden. All much to the tremendous never allowed to be forgotten amusement of another local gardener now working a couple of houses along. Did I feel foolish!

Many a mickle

As I mentioned there was not much profit to be made on turf, though the laying of it was conveniently better done at those times of year when other work could be short. It also could bring in other work, paths and borders and so on all of which added more value to the job. Even so as plants, just like turf and all the other materials are sold so cheaply in garden centres and now on-line so it's always been hard to make much of a margin on those. Unless you buy in bulk when it becomes more lucrative, but that means a lorry load which may take some time to shift.

One of the more profitable jobs I'd most enjoy was advising folk on how to run their gardens themselves, not more efficiently as they asked but more effectively, which they needed much more. I had run several evening classes on gardening in some nearby towns and picked up some consultations from these. Quite a few were from folk who had retired from city life to the country and were planning on enjoying their new much larger gardens. However often then finding they could not keep up with them, even with paid help. Then many turned to a common error, they imagined they could pay for the help by selling, usually herbs, at the garden gate. It was not comfortable to disillusion them however garden gate sales cannot support much at all. The problem is, you've moved to the country, so even in a busy village the foot-fall is small, the passing traffic is light and thus the number of prospective customers tiny. And worse, if you sell eggs there is the likelihood of regular repeat business, but sell rosemary and lavender plants...

Then they stray even further from grim reality when they blithely suggest they might sell their plants to local garden centres and shops to sell on. Even if they could match the quality and presentation of the commercial competition did they have any idea of the wholesale discount? Whereas you might get a couple of quid for a lavender plant from a passing sale which is pure profit at first as you use pots that are to hand and hand written labels. Wholesale you'll only get tens of pence per plant. And when you sell wholesale the number means you now need buy pots, labels and commercial compost, and trays to hold the pots, and transport to the garden centres.

Now I don't want to put off anyone considering a horticultural business but there is a huge leap from amateur gardening production methods to competitive commercial ones, a situation even talented people find difficult to cope with. There are profits to be made but these are small until the turnover becomes huge.

There are however possibilities of profit for the jobbing , gardener with cooperative clients. If you buy plants to fill client's borders you can make a mark up, a small percentage profit, maybe with a trade discount on top you can make say 30%, but if you grew those plants yourself you would make near 100% profit. Now many shrubs are easy to propagate from cuttings- which of course you have pruned from other customer's gardens and been paid to take away. Likewise herbaceous plants often benefit from being dug up every few years with the best pieces from the outside of the clump replanted. A rewarding winter's task, plus of course you charge for taking away the unused bits, which you promptly plant in your own garden to bulk up then sell. Or even more efficiently take to plant up in another customer's garden straight away, at that time of the year it's only the label that shows!

One cunning local gardener had long been a supplier to myself and other smaller businesses. He seemed to have a surprising range of plants available in quite large numbers, but only ever 'bare rooted' in the dormant season, seldom potted. More oddly he always so helpfully brought them to me, he would drop them off wrapped in newspaper and always freshly dug, in itself a sign of good quality. I offered to collect but he always insisted. Finally from another gardener I learnt his secret, he hardly had much garden of his own but he'd worked out which customers of his barely noticed their gardens as long as they were neat and tidy. He had then utilised their beds and borders, even adding new ones, in gardens all over the area as his own private nursery to multiply and bulk up a multitude of the commoner plants he'd worked out he could easily sell.

When I told him I knew his secret he was not perturbed, after all his clients were satisfied, and did not we all filch cuttings and offsets?

Anyway as he pointed out he was only doing the same as so-and-so, a local exponent at the time of evergreen and dwarf conifer gardens. This style was much about the relative size, shape and proportion of these plants. Not really sympathetic with country farmhouses, more a match for Nordic wooden chalets, or concrete bunkers. Now even slow growing dwarf conifers still grow. Thus after a few years many became too big to sit beside the 'rock', water feature or whatever, and thus 'needed' to be replaced by younger more compact and just like the original versions. And of course the superseded specimens dug out would be 'thrown in' the back of the truck to be disposed of. Nope, they were just refreshed and sold on to another customer who had a slightly larger position needing filling. And so on, my informant reckoned he'd heard this old boy boast he'd sold one set of dwarf conifers four times to four different customers over a couple of decades.

Mind you, though that might have been cunning it was effectively legitimate business practice. I was less impressed by another who reckoned he'd extracted the full waste disposal fee for a truck load of concrete slabs he'd been paid to clear, and which he'd already sold, and laid, for another client.

Golden tip
It's hard to make money gardening or selling whatever you grow. I'd not recommend it as a living but it can furnish some pocket money. If you want to sell from your garden gate there are a couple of things you might try. Forget most fruit and vegetables, and common garden plants, all are so inexpensive to buy anyway, and even when you have a surplus it takes time and effort for them to then earn very little. Sell Courgettes, oh come on, don't make me die laughing. Apples, they will have to be for free to shift many at all.

Better offer the more unusual, in a short trial hot pepper plants out sold tomato plants 5:1. Choice fruits, particularly bunches of grapes, will sell, and bags of nuts go remarkably well, especially running up to Christmas.

Most of all though offer what makes you more profit per sale for your effort, bunches of beautiful cut flowers earn far more than sacks full of spuds or carrots, and are much less onerous to pick.

Early, and it has to be early, Daffodils go, just like that, in bunches of a dozen in full bud, don't sell for much but are guaranteed. Then later, bunches of Sweet peas likewise, bought almost as soon as you put them out. Do not forget- just before Valentine's and Mother's days is the time to put on sale any flowers, plants, candles, soaps etc you have, in particular nice looking houseplants will make a premium.

For a houseplant impulse sale you cannot beat the Parrot plant Impatiens congolensis (name now changed but I prefer this old one). This is an easily multiplied Busy Lizzie relative with incredible yellow and red plastic looking parrots for flowers. Of course you can only sell so many at any place and time once everyone has got one.

A good regular, grow your own profit scheme is cultivate Christmas trees. These cost a few pence apiece for seedlings becoming sellable as small trees in only a few years. They're worth more grown for their last year in plastic pots or even bags to sell as rooted trees. And if you are foresighted and have improved any customers' gardens by planting well fed and watered variegated and berrying hollies and ivies then you'll also have seasonal decorative 'prunings' to sell with your trees.

(Mistletoe though profitable in theory is notoriously difficult to get to grow anywhere you want it. However because of the potential easy sale for mistletoe it's well worth trying. Best leave the berries to ripen on the sprigs in a cool light place till March, then simply smear seeds into shallow slits in bark of the prospective host trees such as apple and poplar.)

If it's not nailed down

Although I once thought I had a lawn stolen the worry was not unfounded because I'd had newly planted plants pulled up and taken, and not so rarely. In any garden open to or easily accessible from the road it became necessary to take photos of the finished job to prove you had planted the area, and especially of any valuable hardware you had installed. Seats, benches, vases, all could walk overnight. York paving was the most worrying, it's damned expensive yet easy to lift and take away unless concreted down rather than just laid on sand. Bizarrely new hedges seemed especially at risk, which is plain silly as young hedge plants are so ridiculously inexpensive it's crass effort to steal them. (You will be amazed by the low price apiece if you buy by the score or more.)

One client had a well loved, not valuable, concrete urn full of flowering bulbs which stood on three bricks in a blocked off doorway at the front of their house. This had little intrinsic value yet was stolen fairly regularly, though then only making it a little way along the road when it became too heavy to lug further. However this was becoming irksome so I was asked to fix it in place with a chain. My aesthetics rebelled, a chain hanging off it would look so naff, or at least the quality of chain and fixings they suggested would. Then a friend suggested a cunning plan. First I was to drill a hole through the concrete underneath where the pot stood to hold an expanding bolt set in the concrete. To this was to be fitted a short chain, fixing the other end to a bolt through the bottom of the urn, importantly leaving no more than a few inches of slack which would then be hidden out of sight by the supporting bricks when the urn was in place. Seemed a good idea so the urn had the chain and bolts fitted and was set back in position resting on the three bricks and refilled. It worked brilliantly. From then on the urn stayed put, or rather was sometimes found dislodged though never gone. The cunning and vicious twist was it could be lifted up, at that point the idiots will have thought they were having away their heist, when the chain will have abruptly stopped their hoist dead. Should have done their backs a power of good every time!

When does insurance pay?
Unfortunately early on in almost the first week of my business I had had all my favourite tools on board when my vehicle was stolen. Now I had been sensible and taken out several insurance policies, Public Liability and Road Traffic being indispensable, and had also been persuaded to take out cover for my Trade Tools though I'd never expected to need to make a claim nor so soon. However neither had the insurance agents who thought they smelt a rat and so played up. When I walked in to claim I had not even received the confirmation by mail of the policy they had sold me, things moved slowly back then. They were not happy. First they told me my tools were insured ONLY when locked in the vehicle IN a locked garage or under

supervision of a watchman. Indeed I would not even have been covered if I was using them at the time and certainly not when left in the vehicle at night. I protested they had not said that when selling me the policy! I was going to go to get legal help! They asked me to wait, then they muttered a bit and took the papers into the back office, out of sight. Shortly they returned saying they'd looked into it more closely and explained I was not insured because I had opted for an exclusion for high risk areas, so the policy did not cover me at all as I had been away from my local area visiting a girlfriend in North London. Originally they had filled in the paperwork with me and as it was so recent I remembered well and was fairly sure I'd not wanted that or any other exclusion -expecting much of my more lucrative work might be with city friends. They triumphantly showed me a tick in a box on the paperwork –this act in itself looked suspicious, and to my jaundiced eye the ink looked like it had only just been done.

I took legal advice, which was morally on my side but pointed out I had no chance as the 'evidence' was in their favour so it was just my word against theirs. Needless to say I did not use the same agents again, indeed I stopped taking almost any insurance not legally necessary. I'm sorry to say it seems much insurance is a scam, they sell the idea of cover when in practice if it is needed you are left to cope unaided. That company did not last long, as I said you can't behave like that in a country area where we pass on local knowledge / gossip.

My own parents were appallingly badly served, a digression.
They had been with the same insurance company for more than forty years and never made a claim. Then their living room floor unexpectedly dropped and tilted. A leaking central heating pipe under the floor had slowly washed away the sandy soil of the hill the house stood upon until becoming unsupported the weight of the concrete slab floor caused it to tilt and drop. This of course then stressed the pipe connections creating greater leakage that soon threatened the walls' stability as the floor shifted more. The house was deemed unsafe until everything was rectified, which would be straightforward if expensive, and the insurance company tried to deny responsibility claiming ridiculous reasons why. My elderly parents were forced to live in a caravan parked on their driveway, right into and through the winter months. The insurance company continually weaseled, refusing to settle, for month after month. The winter weather was hard on my parents trying to cope in a caravan. But no movement from the insurance company with their refusing to accept responsibility for what was manifestly exactly the sort of thing folk take out insurance for! It was hardly a fraud by my parents, a fire with the loss of valuable possessions may be suspiciously arranged but subsidence! The cost of repairs was too large for my parents to find themselves and things looked hopeless. In

the end I contacted the company -through their public relations department under the guise of writing for a newspaper (which was true even if on horticulture) asking for a quote for that and a well known TV consumer show (the same one I had threatened the chemist with over the strychnine licence). I had their attention: this was going to be very bad publicity for them, my mother was registered disabled, both parents retired pensioners, and they'd been good customers for four decades. Their house had become unlivable through no fault of their own, not an act of God as purported but a plain simple leak... Would they like to explain their logic on this? The workmen arrived very soon after.

Strange goings on
An odd thing took place while I was working in one deserted garden. I had been called for 'tidying' up a long neglected overgrown garden to subdue it into some semblance of neatness as the house was to be rented out. This house was Victorian, huge, with a dozen or more rooms and obviously most had not been lived in for a long while. Seems an old lady had finally departed after having been barely noticeable for decades.

The garden must once have been lovely but had grown unkempt, this appeared rather appealing to my eyes but everything was requiring a 'ruthless prune' to the newly inherited owners who wanted it 'tidy enough' to rent out a.s.a.p. This kept me busy for many pleasant days on and off over many weeks, the 'lawns' were slowly mown into submission, the formal hedges and shrubs trimmed and pruned and a collapsed rose arbor slowly resurrected. A dilapidated conservatory / greenhouse was tidied and a few surviving succulents rescued (bringing with them a mass of Mealy bugs pretending to be part of a fluffy cactus) along with a 'wooden brick'. This turned out to be the biggest tuber of Mirabilis jalapa (Marvel of Peru, pretty, scented, houseplant) I've ever seen. Seems it had found the conditions of a leaky draughty glasshouse perfect and given decades of uninhibited growth what would usually grow as large as an apple had become a venerable shoebox sized relic. Marginally tender I gave this home in my polytunnel where sadly I lost it, not from cold but moisture, the conditions were too damp with winter rotting it away from underneath.

Anyway as the weeks passed my visits continued, this job was regular work and as not yet rented so with no-one at home it was easy to fit into a difficult schedule, often finishing there last thing at dusk. Now I'm sceptical and not at all worried about ghosts, ghouls, duppies or whatever, I'm no more uncomfortable in a graveyard at night than anywhere else. Though there was a decided atmosphere around this old place this did not bother me, I just carried on, though with that odd feeling of being watched. I was cutting the 'lawns' when I was first spooked, out of the corner of my eye I saw something in an upstairs window. It seemed as if someone with white hair and face had been looking down at me. I ignored this as one does, saying to myself it was just a reflection on the window pane. Till it happened again, only this time I was at a different angle so it was unlikely reflections. Well then, must be intruders, not unlikely, empty houses in the country are often stripped of copper pipe and wire. Though there was scant amounts of either- this old mansion had electric lights of the earliest fitting and I believe only one power socket in the entire place, the plumbing was equally archaic limited to one toilet, one bath and a sink in the kitchen scullery. When someone did rent the house it was a chap bringing his large family from overseas. He was not exactly amused by the inordinate lack of facilities. Indeed I'm not sure there was even any heating as such other than fireplaces in every room. Which turned out to have been the cause of my apparition. Having gone inside and upstairs to find the room where I had thought I'd seen someone I entered bravely, trusty hoe in hand just in case. And left amused, after letting out a pigeon that had fallen down the chimney, it was this I had seen fluttering at the window.

With some relief I returned to my work. One of the tasks here was to reduce the overgrown herbage along the drive verges, it was uneven and a lawnmower could not be safely driven over such terrain. In these places a nylon line trimmer known as a Strimmer, was handy. Powered by a very noisy two stroke motor this has a viciously spinning nylon wire blade on a short pole. With this evil weapon you could slice down nettles, brambles and soft growths reducing them to shreds. Superb for tidying an , area though harsh on wild life, risky to the bark on trees and so on, and very dirty and noisy. So with boots, gloves, overalls, Balaclava helmet over the head and face, staring through misted up goggles I'd move methodically along swinging this whirring blade rhythmically to some tune, often Glen Millers' In the Mood (which oddly was from way before my time).

Now I used this strimmer often, it was one of my most useful tools. It was a pain being swaddled up but necessary as the flying debris would coat me with bits and the odd thorn, piece of woody material or small stone could penetrate like shrapnel. And I was used to working alongside roads with traffic, the habit was to pause so as not to be accused of pelting folk with stones and fallacious claims for damage or injury. Out of the corner of my eye I'd see the movement (no chance of hearing anything) and promptly lift the blade moving it and me away from whatever I was cutting till the traffic had passed then continue. And all in time to the music in my head.

Anyway I was on full automatic, blithely strimming the verge along the driveway where it wound through the shrubberies. Without missing a beat I stepped off the drive up onto the verge to let the coach and horses past then resumed cutting. A second later I went WHAT! I'd just moved out of the way to let a coach and horses past-who had manifestly not been there when I arrived.

I had been working there for some hours and no-one had been about nor down the drive nor out on the road. They had appeared just as any car or truck would have, solely in the corner of my eye, I'd never looked directly. I'm not sure I believe these things exist out there but more likely are inside us. Made an impression on me though, not scary, just odd, and to this day every time I drive past that mansion I stare down the drive weirly hoping to catch sight again of that ephemeral coach and horses.

Missing a friend
As I said I'm skeptical, I do not believe in ghosts as such nor indeed in almost anything I cannot weigh, measure or reproduce. But I do not dis-believe either, even the craziest idea, cult or sect might, just might, be valid, though I doubt it. However I consider many things we do not yet understand may appear to us conflated in our minds with what we already expect. That distant animal on the side of the road turns out to be a bush or a fluttering plastic bag. Folk have always seen 'things' in the sky, once they were Angels and now Flying Saucers. (Suggest you read the Book of the Damned by Charles Fort, 1919, he shows folk saw balloons, then aircraft, in the skies before any recorded at all in those places, and all this was happening many decades before UFOs were first

reported.) Anyway, I am sure we may mistake, miss-take, what is going on, even creating an event through misperception. Nonetheless one day I I saw someone who was not, could not be, there.

One of my friends charmingly called Arabella Aphrodite Seeds, a name not easily forgotten, unfortunately had Cystic Fibrosis, a difficult health issue. Thus although still mobile she was weak and unable to carry on much active gardening herself though loving it. We belonged to a local gardening group and as a trip we had organised a Sunday afternoon visit to Chelsea Physic Garden in London which had just been re-discovered. (An interesting place, a very old botanic garden on the bank of the Thames set up to provide medicinal plants for the hospital. When potions were replaced by pills and when the NHS was created this garden carried on as it had been, just no one knew of it other than as a bureaucratic item. It's said it was only when the last gardener died and needed replacement someone asked the question and they found out they had this amazing green oasis right in the middle of London.)

Still, back to that Sunday afternoon. Along with several other car loads from the group Arabella was coming on this trip and I looked forward to seeing her there. Though at the start she had still not arrived, but then it's a long journey, the garden really was a secret place back then and parking was little easier then as now. It was a lovely day and we had split into several small groups investigating the different sections when I spotted Arabella walking with another group across the end of some beds a short distance away. I broke off and walked around to that group, but she was no longer with them so I trotted off in the direction she had been going. I quartered the garden, and again, then started asking folk if they'd seen her and where she'd gone. Oddly none of them had noticed her arrive though she had been expected, she was quite well known with distinctive looks and a strikingly abundant head of hair. The garden was not that large but was full, even congested, with lush plants and shrubs so it would be easy enough to miss someone in the passing. Anyway it was a busy afternoon and a long trip back so I thought maybe she'd come late and then probably left again shortly after as lacking the stamina. It was only when I returned home I received the message Arabella had collapsed and died earlier that day, she'd never even left home.

I still remember her often and am grateful for the curved metal support frames for my first polytunnel which she gave me when she'd had to give up gardening herself. They had been a great gift if awkward to handle. Ungainly to move these large semi-circular metal tube arches had perched upside down in my car trailer threatening to impale passing strangers as they wobbled about on the journey home. It's handy to live in a country area with quiet back roads as that was one of the least-safe loads

I've ever been party to.

Mad as a tree surgeon
Health & Safety had not laid its heavy hand too closely on us back then. Plus, as the famous phrase goes- I was young and foolish, and needed the money. Anyway I was overhauling an overgrown orchard, mostly removing congested and dead wood. A task I relished as although hard work it is pleasing work to prune, and a bonfire was such legitimate fun in those innocent days (and the ash well worth having for it's potash content). Anyway, trimming this orchard of old trees was almost finished save for the tallest. It was also near un-climbable so most of the light work would be with the long arm pruner (a ten foot long pole with a blade at the top operated by a lever at the bottom) and heavier branches sawn with another pole with a saw on top. I had an excellent though ancient set of tall wooden steps, solid, heavy and stable to stand on. Of course on rough turf you need to place pads under the feet to keep this level and to stop it rocking. I used wooden pallets as these were effective and gave a bit more height. But often this was still too short. So I had a heavy duty plastic beer crate which would sit on top of the steps giving an extra foot or two of lift.

Anyway having removed all dead wood within reach there was still more higher up, and which was too obvious to leave. So desperate to get the job done by the fading light of the wintry afternoon I drove my old Volvo estate underneath. I put the pallets onto the car's roof (where two roof racks held them up in place and six inches higher still) and managed to lift the heavy steps up into position atop those. This gave me much more height, another five or six feet, brilliant. Unfortunately of course the car shifted on its suspension with my weight making the stepladder sway alarmingly. So I clambered down and rammed a couple of logs under the car's sills till it was wedged solid. Getting back up I near finished the pruning, save for one last manky looking branch which was beyond reach even at full stretch. I came down, thought about it, failed to think about it enough as I so wanted to get done, and so went back up with the beer crate. Putting this on top the steps, on top the pallets, on top the roof racks of the estate car resting on logs I then slowly, tremulously, got up on top myself, now more than a little apprehensive. The heft of a ten foot wooden pruner being waved around is hard enough to manage when standing on solid ground. I was way up wobbling on mine own gallows when I felt the pole going over, I could not stop it or I would be unbalanced further and then fall for sure. It came down in an arc like a battle axe, straight into my windscreen where it embedded itself. Interesting shaped hole to explain, at the garage said a falling piece of tree caused the damage, seemed near enough to the truth without the embarrassment...

Flying stones gather no moss

Of course gardening can involve broken glass too easily, especially with power tools such as mowers or strimmers which can flick a stone viciously in any direction. I used to wear football shin-pads inside my overalls when I had a lot of strimming to do, especially if that was on 'dirty' ground (gravel, litter, plastic, glass and tins all hide in long grass and weeds). And of course for comfort as much as safety a full head covering and or mask and goggles. However one foolish day it was so warm and sunny I left off the Balaclava while I was trimming along a fence by a road, singing joyfully with the rhythm of the work. That was added foolishness. I saw it coming but as with so many accidents it was too fast occurring and I was powerless to stop in time. A large dock leaf, which if I'd thought for a moment looked suspiciously wilted and oddly flat on the ground, was being whipped aside by my madly spinning cutting line as this then chewed down into the large fat brown dog turd it had concealed underneath. Too late, a thousand splatters were flung all over my legs and front, into my mouth, up my nose. Oh that was disgusting, so disgusting. Weirdly I agreed some time later to have this whole incident re-created, with a chocolate brownie substitute, for a TV program warning about gardening accidents. Fame comes in strange ways.

Stinks, there are worse

Yet even nastier if you can conceive it, was the time when strimming round an overgrown pond I burst upon an entire clutch of rotten duck eggs, which immediately exploded like a bunch of grenades. I was instantly, multiply, coated from top to wellies. With little hesitation I threw myself into the pond just to get as much of the disgusting stuff off as fast as I could, but even after returning home (driving near naked) for a shower and change of clothes that awful taint lingered on for days.

There is something really unpleasant about the stench from rotten eggs, as a friend's young daughter discovered. She was staying over a weekend and had come with me to feed the hens and collect the eggs. While being shown the nest boxes where they laid I had taken a China egg (made of pottery these lure the hens to lay in the 'right' place) and pretended to try and smash it on top of my head before revealing it was made of clay. As hoped this caused some amusement. The next day she came again this time bringing her mother, she wanted to show her mother the hens and where we collected eggs. Unfortunately mistaking an old egg in the straw on the floor for one of the China eggs she thought she'd be clever and show her mother the same trick. Need I say more, it exploded at the first tap coating her, her mother and I, and the inside of the henhouse, with splatter of the most obnoxious sort. Okay we laughed about it later though at the time it was so disgusting.

Feather dust
One day I was called to price up, and gained, a valuable

gardening contract to maintain the grounds of a local factory, one that made pillows, duvets and similar products. One whose frontage sward glowed an emerald green amongst duller neighbours. Having worked in several nearby gardens I knew how poor was this sandy soil yet here it produced abundant growth, rather more than a man with a prospective grass-cutting contract really wanted to see. Now I could understand grassed areas might have been fertilised by a previous contractor (as I noted, even if not part of the job it was worth feeding and watering sward so as to ensure it would continue growing strongly and thus obviate any ideas of laying off the grass cutting through droughts. But this seemed on steroids and as a contractor myself I knew no-one would feed a client's grass with more than the minimum required, after all it's business and fertiliser costs dear. Moreover it was not just the grass that grew so lush, everything all round was growing far too well. Even weeds on the overgrown back lots were way above head height and nobody would ever have bothered to have fed those.

Then it struck me, after all it was not difficult to work out the reason. This company handled massive quantities of feathers from the many local poultry farms and processing factories. Feathers are mostly made of protein so have a high fertility value (in horticultural terms they contain around 15% Nitrogen). Daily truckloads full of newly plucked feathers arrived to be industrially washed, dried, fluffed up, graded and bagged in the main factory. In surrounding buildings some of these processed feathers were packed into pillows, cushions, duvets and so on. Despite all due care over the many decades minor sprays, drips, dusts and spillages from all of these had contributed a fine dressing of feathers big, small and particles, all around onto the surrounding site. Mostly unseen and inoffensive this feather dust was no problem, and the natural processes were using this new resource to grow more lushly. I would have to cut the sward more frequently and it would be harder work but hey, at least I would not have to expend any margin on fertiliser. And I could see another advantage. Chatting with the owner I'd discovered they regularly paid to dispose of quantities of feather waste, a gritty dust sieved from the dried washed feathers. Willing to take away the same for free I thought I'd try this out on my own sward, and then possibly those of other clients at a potentially huge profit.

So we come to the second part of this story. Feather dust was an odd material, difficult to handle it flew about on any breeze. Also hard to wet the stuff turned out better suited for mixing into potting composts rather than broadcasting about. Quantities of feather waste also proved to be rather too rich for most crops, however blackcurrants appreciate such very rich fertility. Thus one day I was shoveling barrow loads of this stuff which I was getting for free under my bushes while hosing it down to keep it in place. I do admit some was blowing about, well lots, but I'd checked (as before a bonfire) to be sure no neighbour had washing out drying on their line. Unfortunately one neighbour, an elderly widow, pleasant enough but an inveterate prolific and repetitive whinger, was rushing down her path towards our common fence and myself obviously about to protest about this dusty stuff blowing into her garden. I prepared for her deluge of complaints, followed by repeat performances every time I was sighted, at least until her next 'cause celebre'. (She had recently tried to involve me in a dispute with another neighbour whose trees were shading her garden or so she claimed, a difficult argument to get to grips with as they grew on her Northern side!) Now I don't know where my response came from, it just popped into my head, but as I started to apologise for the fluffy stuff blowing about I found myself saying I was "trying out a new mulch" and somehow instead of 'Feather dust' it came out as "Asbestos waste from Sizewell Nuclear Power station". (This is close by on our coast, locally pronounced as Sizzle). It was, well, explosive, she stopped in her tracks as if I'd slapped her, retreated hurriedly back indoors and drew the curtains tight shut. Indeed it was many months before I saw her again and so had opportunity to explain.

I knew that stuff would come in useful one way or another.

Go the extra mile

The same feather factory was the site of another uplifting experience. As noted above this was a maintenance contract, I had to keep the grounds neat and tidy for a fixed fee per month. Hard work whenever the grass grew so strongly but in East Anglia for many months it's so dry the grass grows but little even when over-fertilised with feather dust. However there's still litter to pick and any sward still needs mowing despite the drought to prevent weeds producing seed heads and tussock grasses dominating. Anyway, it was a hot summer's morning, workers had started on a new building going up next door, some folk were working away inside the factory but all was tranquil as I unloaded my massive mower to start cutting. This was antiquated, loud and fearsomely effective, a powerful six and a half horsepower engine (don't forget a 2CV car has much less) with a three speed gearbox, even a disc brake! I walked the grounds picking litter, moving errant stones preparing for the mowing which was done most expeditiously by first cutting the difficult corners and perimeter then the bulk could be done in unimpeded back and forth slices. With only a light trim required I could use the faster second speed instead of the usual slow but sure crawler, third gear was special and was not for cutting but for faster travel moving the mower between areas. Now this was not a ride on but a walk behind, you steered by pushing down on the handle lifting the front end and heaving the machine pointing which ever way you wanted as the front wheels came down again. Physical effort but okay, with co-ordination as you had to simultaneously pull the clutch to stop the back wheels pulling the mower out from under you of course.

I was mowing away and all was fine and dandy as I completed the fiddly bits with the bulk left, I'd just started doing the long back and forth runs when a crunch happened, an aged bracket came away from it's weld and the pulley it held flew off. Repairable, but not in the field, worse I could hardly leave the job so obviously unfinished so I was going to have to load up, go home unload, and promptly turn around and return with the back up mower. And that was much smaller so would take three times as long to cut the last piece. In desperation I conceived a bodge, in complete breach of common sense and safety regulations, but it would get me out of the quandary. I could pervert the now too slack drive belt to go round the third gear 'fast' pulley and also 'illegally' spun the blade's pulley at the same time, something it was never intended to do. This bodge re-positioning the belt would however mean the clutch could not be operated, so as soon as the engine turned the blades would spin the wheels turn and the mower would lurch off. This would be with both the blades whizzing round over-speed and the mower moving at a very fast pace. There would be no way of stopping other than cutting the engine, the brake had no chance with that powerful engine at full pelt.

When needs must the devil drives.

I foolishly started. As I pulled the cord the engine fired and the mower ran away from me, frantically I grabbed the handle to be dragged along, as it reached the headland I managed to lift the rear driving wheels off the ground, swing the machine round and drop those now over-revving wheels with a huge jerk and an even rougher wrench pulling me along behind on the return trip. Back and forth I tore, hanging on as the machine rushed up and down with excruciatingly difficult turns at each end till eventually I'd mowed the last swathe and cut the engine. The glorious silence was immediately broken by applause, whistling, cat calls and laughter. I turned, to see a dozen or so guys from the building site next door staring down from atop their scaffolding. One shouted out

"We have a bet- you're self employed aren't you?"

Hoisted on his own petard
Sometimes you get one back. Sadly too often you think of the response after the worthy recipient has departed but this time I got a direct hit without any delay with a wonderfully quick retort to a local Grinch. This grouse had a dour sense of humour, or rather put downs, which he dished out at every opportunity: "You've missed a bit up there", "That was looking okay till you fixed it", "My dog would have done a better job"...

He wandered up one morning as I was unloading sacks of

manure from my trailer. I seldom brought in manure but wanted some for a hotbed experiment, I'd filled these at a nearby farm fattening bullocks for slaughter as that was extra rich stuff. He stopped and watched my labour, which in itself was an annoying trait. As I barrowed the heavy sacks past he quipped

" So what you got there for me, anything I could use?"

Out of the blue I heard my response

"Bull-shit, but you'd not be needing any more of that!"

He sloped off, well trounced.

A rose by any other name
A family had me maintain their garden, which seemed they regarded as little more than an out-door room mostly used for barbecues. It had a length of ancient hedge, some grassed sward, a remnant of orchard and a once proud shrubbery set around an old farmhouse. My remit was to keep this all trim and tidy, no problem, and no disrespect, each to their own.

Thus I was a tad surprised when I was asked to look at their Rosemary as apparently it had something wrong with it. Umm, I did not recall any Rosemary, and was further amazed they knew Rosemary as till then they had displayed a complete lack of interest or knowledge about anything in the garden beyond my maintaining it in respectably neat tidiness.

The mother explained; her family loved their grandmothers' roast lamb rubbed with honey, salt and Rosemary but they did not like it when she made the same at home, even when following instructions to the letter. Perhaps something was wrong with their Rosemary?

She led me around the corner to the back of the house, I was perplexed, I was sure there was no Rosemary anywhere there. A glimmer of an idea; maybe she had bought some in a pot? She walked up to and stood in front of, a huge old Lavender bush, obviously awaiting my prognosis. It was an easy mistake if you know neither well, how embarrassed she must have felt. Still no harm done, after all I enjoy Lavender shortbread and Lavender rice so Lavendered lamb would be another, shall we say, unusual delicacy. They became much happier with the authentic taste of Rosemary from some lovely new bushes I planted along the sunny front of the house soon after.

Be warned
Of course as a gardener you are always being asked to identify this or that tree, plant or natural curiosity. It goes with the territory, I just give thanks I never chose to become a dentist, chiropodist or proctologist.

Problem is even a very experienced gardener may not be an accomplished botanist (while many pundits have even less qualification). There are tens of thousands of different varieties and species of plants in cultivation to say little of the native weeds, trees and shrubs. No-one can possibly know them all to identify.

Beware as you get to know the commoner ones you may feel emboldened. Never be too quick to identify plants! You may be fairly sure one in front of you is X however as you familiarize yourself with even more plants you may realise it is not the commonplace X but Y, Z or Ω, all of which can look awfully similar but not quite the same in some small detail. It is especially risky when you only have some of the clues such as leaf, bark and form, when you also have the flower and fruit or seed it becomes surer.

The danger as I said is being too quick to identify a specimen, if you name it correctly all well and good. But if you get it wrong then you have just shown you don't really know that plant in front of you, AND neither do you really know the plant you just wrongly thought it was.

However whether you got it right or wrong there's a good chance they will probably not remember it correctly either anyway unless you write it down for them...

Also, beware of believing labels, even in Botanic gardens, as these may have been moved inadvertently or even deliberately. If wishing to be sure of an ID they will probably have a catalogue and plan which can be double checked. (The internet now offers remarkably good IDs from photos although it is also prone to error, an old fashioned reference book is a good investment.)

(At this point it might be a good idea to draw a map or plan of your own garden writing the names of known subjects, most especially the long lived or important to know such as fruit trees. Make a copy and nail that to a rafter in your attic as a note for posterity.)

Garden centres and nurseries may or may not be reliable as to their labelling, generally most try but some errors always happen, most often in the 'remainders' area. Although honesty is good policy unscrupulous traders have given horticulture the saying that 'a lie is a plant description often used for convenience to make a sale'.

Thus to summarise the above, it is hard to be sure of any plant ID, not just from the actual identification but also as that employed for comparison may itself be doubtful. Even more so when your experience is without having grown an example yourself. If you've grown it you know it. Rather like your own children you can instantly tell them apart from a thousand others.

One gambit you can sometimes get away with though is indicating a plant while saying "Now exactly which species / variety do we have here?" or even better "Have you grown this from seed or is it a named variety?" Either said with blithe confidence will infer you are completely cognizant of the Genus.

Feather in my cap

A few gardeners even have a tricky plant they deliberately employ to test other gardeners' veracity. Whilst leading you around they will pause in front of it and ask some vague questions to feel you out. This is not the time to blather or bluff. If you know a plant be confident if not admit it. Do not be so foolish as to take a flying guess, you will be shot down in flames, not just then but at every opportunity they have thereafter. As I said it really is the case of if you've grown it you know it.

My greatest 'victory' was whilst attending a rather grand event in a marquee in the grounds of a great house. Having arrived in good time I was relaxing in the Green Room (tent) when I was invited by the hereditary retainer whether I would like to see his Arboretum (collection of trees). With time to spare I was pleased to accompany on a jaunt so we set off in a golf buggy to see many acres of mostly, to me not very interesting, species of Oaks. Then we came to the edge of a clearing where we pulled up by a smaller somewhat Ash like tree. It was obvious I was being tested even though nought was being said, we just sat there looking at it in silence.

The branches were slender, upright, arching over, the foliage Ash like in form but finer, more Rowan like. Indeed as there are so many Sorbus in cultivation one of these would have been a good bet. However this was a much rarer specimen, very unusual, so unusual that when I recounted this anecdote to the great plants-man Roy Lancaster he confirmed he'd only seen a handful during his entire travels and few of those in the UK.

If it had been in flower it would have been easy as those are resplendent as glorious as Horse chestnut blooms though along the stems not on candles. And this trees' seed pods really are most distinctive, large green cases, oddly opening in a peculiar triangular form, to drop or rather fling in the wind, round (edible, which is why I grew it) seeds like small black marbles. No remains of these were present which indicated to me the specimen though mature was not awfully happy.

This tree, Xanthoceras, has long been recorded in gardening 'bibles' as 'thick fleshy yellow roots take kindly to a chalk formation' which I believe is a misprint for 'do not take kindly to' as when I tried growing from seed I found these only germinated well in Ericaceous composts -which is a bit of a give away. This error may have come about by conflation with the next entry for another plant, Xanthorrhiza simplicissima, Yellow-root, which has the advice "Thrives in moist clayey soil but is not at home in a shallow chalk soil."

Over many decades I've only seen a couple of other Xanthoceras other than my own, both were doing well and both were in wet, leaf mold rich, low lime, garden situations. I suspect the reason this tree is so scarce is simply because it does not like dry soils with much lime, which immediately rules out many UK gardens.

Anyway back to my anecdote; I was confident, very confident. I had grown these from seed all the way to maturity. I knew them as well as I knew my own kids. I turned to his Lordship and said

"Your Xanthoceras sorbifolium, Yellow Horn, looks like it could do with a thick mulch of leaf mold to perk it up, your soils probably too dry and too lime rich for it (remember this was an Oak arboretum), I'd be surprised if it's ever cropped, has it even flowered?"

He was crest fallen, I'd not failed nor bluffed, he'd apparently had the pleasure of catching out so many but I'd nailed it. It turned out I was the first visitor in over forty years to have recognised this unusual Chinese tree.

I was so chuffed, I'd won real respect there.

This pat on the back occurred some years after I joined the panel of Gardener's Question Time, which along with my writing and public speaking has kept me gainfully employed these last decades, fortunately.

For working as a professional gardener had been tough on

my back and joints and became very difficult after I passed sixty years of age. My body was still hard and strong and I loved the outdoor life but the wear and tear had become too much to continue full time. So I retired from active service, no more landscaping or maintenance work and decided to concentrate on writing. And after all I still had a garden of mine own to cherish.

I do miss those days though. It's with some welling of nostalgia I poignantly remember sultry summer afternoons from those more youthful days perfumed by freshly mown grass. Totally absorbed strolling up and down, to and fro behind a purring mower embossing perfectly striped patterns fleetingly across acres of lush green lawn.

As with us; wonderful yet ephemeral as the sandy ripples upon a beach.

Foot-note- My garden is a private garden, it is my laboratory for horticultural exploration, there is no café, gift shop or garden centre here. And because of flagrant breaches of health & safety, lack of insurance, lack of parking and appalling access it is never open to the public. I do not do tours nor have individuals nor groups visit, not for charity, nor even for cash.

If you've an unusual horticultural query you may try me gratis via Twitter / X, but better send it to GQT BBC Radio 4. For a complicated or involved question which requires much consideration then I will point out that as with my dentist, garage and accountant I'm always delighted to take on new and challenging work -but seldom pro bono....

You will find answers to many horticultural questions in my numerous articles in Best of Bob on my website where organic fruit and vegetable, greenhouse and wildlife gardening with a mass of other information is available totally gratis www.bobflowerdew.com

Also, you can find daily photos and notes of whatever I find interesting in my garden (and a few odd opinions; note I don't support any party, nor creed, on Twitter X @FlowerdewBob

Plus, with more than two dozen published books I now produce my own, both as Kindle e-books and old fashioned printed on paper, to purchase these please visit Amazon.

What to do When

Timely notes of monthly tasks in each and every area of the garden, "there's a right time for every job- and it was probably last month", very handy for newer gardeners who are taking it all on the first time, and also for us older hands who are not keeping up as well as we did

Really help your plants

Plants and other plants, their good & bad companions and worst weeds'

Being Volume I of 'Plant Companions and Co-lives' the web of life in the British Isles

An A-Z of wild and garden plants and recorded interactions between these and other plants, effects we need to know about whenever planning or planting our gardens.

Really help Butterflies

Being Volume II of 'Plant Companions and Co-lives'

There's little point planting 'flowers to help butterflies' any more than making the North sea bigger to help cod stocks. We need grow those plants their larvae eat.

This is an A-Z of wild and garden plants and which of our native butterfly caterpillars THEIR FOLIAGE will sustain.

Really help your garden ecology

Being Volume III of 'Plant Companions and Co-lives'

Plants & co-lives; their associated fauna: insects, nematodes, bacteria, fungi large & small & shared viruses. Interactions between our native & garden plants & varied forms of life they coexist with not in volumes I & II.

Really help your crops

An edited compilation of all three volumes above selected for the most important interactions, those with our crop plants. Specifically collated data for gardeners, farmers and horticulturists, improve your profit margins growing the right not wrong plants near or far from each crop

Recycle & Reuse stuff in your garden

My first e-book and best seller, never been printed to save paper, exactly what the cover says; simple garden up-cycling uses for all sorts of waste products and junk.

Grow Your Own Kitchen garden & Pantry

This is invaluable, not just how to grow but all the ways to then store, preserve & process your crops, an essential guide to becoming your own delicatessen.

Greenhouse, cloche and tunnel gardening, Growing under cover

What it says on the cover, the distillation of my forty years of experience of protected cropping, including historical development, ways and means, what you need to consider, what you can grow with practical advice on each.

Pulpit in the potting shed

My 'philosophy' expressed in limerick, verse and song

Collected works over five decades

Fifty essays in rhyme, terse verse & dirty ditties.

A penchant to word play

a foreign county -my AutobyBobraphy

Book one, early years, 1953-65, rural life in the fifties & sixties, remnants of old world now gone,

from farming with horses to space age in one leap, and a school more Gormenghast & Whacko than Hogwarts

Vin Dangereux, Vendange heureuse,

Grape picking in Beaujolais, un Raisin d'etre

-my Autoby**Bob**raphy volume V

Printed in Great Britain
by Amazon